THE SOCIAL WORLD OF BIBLICAL ANTIQUITY SERIES

General Editor
James W. Flanagan

THE EARLY BIBLICAL COMMUNITY IN TRANSJORDAN

ROBERT G. BOLING

The Almond Press · 1988

Published by Almond Press
Editorial direction: David M. Gunn
Columbia Theological Seminary
P.O. Box 520, Decatur
GA 30031, U.S.A.
Almond Press is an imprint of
Sheffield Academic Press Ltd
The University of Sheffield
343 Fulwood Road
Sheffield S10 3BP
England

Typeset by Sheffield Academic Press
and
printed in Great Britain
by Billing & Sons Ltd
Worcester

British Library Cataloguing in Publication Data

Boling, Robert G.
The early biblical community in
Transjordan.—(The Social world of
biblical antiquity series, ISSN 0265
-1408; 6).
1. Jordan—Social life and customs
I. Title II. Series
933 DS154.2

ISBN 1-85075-094-7
ISBN 1-85075-093-9 Pbk

CONTENTS

Preface 7

Introduction
EARLY ISRAEL AND EARLIEST ISRAEL 9

Chapter 1
TRANSITIONS IN OLD TRANSJORDAN 11
- The Farmer and the Shepherd are Brothers 11
- Proliferation of Archaeological Surveys 13
- From Middle Bronze to Late Bronze 17
- Early Iron Age 21
  - Excursus on Cisjordan 22
- Edom and the Deep South 24
- Northern Hejaz and 'Midianite' Pottery 26
- Amman and Vicinity 28
- The Lower Zarqa 30
- South of Amman 30

Chapter 2
THE BIBLICAL TRADITION IN CONTEXT 37
- Transjordan in Recent History Writing 37
- Kingdoms of Sihon and Og 41
  - Excursus on Moab, Land and 'Legitimacy' 52
- Early Israel. Yahwist Newcomers and Village-Farmer Sympathizers 53
- Ethnogenesis? 56
- Tribal History in Archaic Poetry 57

Conclusion 62

Bibliography 65
Index of Biblical References 76
Index of Authors 77
Index of Geographical and Place Names 79

MAPS

1. Transjordan: Three Extensive Surveys 15
   a. Northern Jordan
   b. Moabite Plateau
   c. East Jordan Valley
2. Dam Reservoir Survey Areas 19
3. Hesban Region Survey 31
4. Madaba Plains Project, 1984 33

FIGURES

1. Archaeological Heritage of Jordan, 1973 13
2. Three Major Archaeological Surveys 16
3. Late Bronze and Iron Age: Dam Reservoirs 18
4. Cisjordan Settlements 23
5. Hesban Region Survey 32
6. Madaba Plains Project: Random Sample 34
7. Madaba Plains Project: 55 Sites 34

PREFACE

These pages are the product of research carried out in Jordan during 1984, where the first six months of a study leave were in part supported by appointment as Annual Professor at the American Center of Oriental research (ACOR) in Amman. Extensive travel within Jordan and provision for survey work in the field following that term were generously underwritten by a grant from the National Endowment for the Humanities.

Many persons helped to orient the researcher, both for work in the field and to life in Amman. Thanks are due especially to ACOR's Director, David McCreery, whose knowledge of the land and its antiquities is perhaps only matched by his boundless energy, always available to staff and visiting colleagues. Thanks are due also to Dr Adnan Hadidi, Director of Jordan's Department of Antiquities, and to Dr Cherie Lenzen, for help in ready access to the Department's resources. Professor Gerald Mattingly obligingly supplied data from the Survey of Central Moab, and has continued to express keen interest in the project. Special thanks go to Professor Burton MacDonald for supplying pre-publication pages of his Wadi Hasa Survey report, accompanied by long conversations, in the G. Ernest Wright Library at ACOR and in the field. Association with the staff of the Madaba Plains Project, especially Laurence T. Geraty and Øystein S. LaBianca, has been richly rewarding. Finally, from one family to another, for just plain enduring friendship arising out of a shared interest in the history of his land, I must acknowledge the hospitality and continued interest in the project from Mr Farouk Abujabber.

Robert G. Boling
McCormick Theological Seminary
July 7, 1986

To Jean and our daughters
Gail, Ruth and Martha

INTRODUCTION: EARLY ISRAEL AND EARLIEST ISRAEL

In this essay Early Israel refers to the period from Moses to the establishment of monarchy, at least thirteenth to tenth centuries BCE which saw consolidation of the familiar twelve-tribe tradition in the narrow corridor between the Mediterranean Sea and the Syro-Arabian Desert. The tradition focuses religious loyalty exclusively upon Yahweh, but retains ever afterwards an older divine name, El, in its self-understanding as 'Israel'.

Earliest Israel will, accordingly, be our label for an inter-tribal organization of the pre-Mosaic period.

The essay falls in two parts. In Chapter 1, a brief summary of earlier scholars' historical 'conclusions' introduces a survey and summary of archaeological evidence for demographic patterns in ancient Transjordan, from the end of the Middle Bronze Period to the beginning of Iron I, as complete as we could make it, through the 1984 field season. Chapter 2 re-examines pertinent biblical texts concerning the early biblical community in Transjordan, and recent interpretations of them, against the archaeological background.

To anyone familiar with the subject, the quest for a clear view of Early Israel (to say nothing of Earliest Israel) has been exceedingly tortuous. The quest has not been made any easier by the rapid escalation of archaeological work on both sides of the Jordan river, to judge from the papers and discussion at the recent international congress (Biran 1985: esp. pp. 31-95). Nor has the quest been made any easier by a theory recently launched, that would lower the end of the Middle Bronze Period so as to accommodate a fifteenth-century date for the Exodus event (Bimson 1981). This latter new attempt to redefine the MB/LB transition is encountering awesome headwinds from experienced field archaeologists (Callaway 1981).

At the opposite pole of the critical enterprise, the eminent historian of ancient Israel, Martin Noth, and many followers, have long since concluded that the quest for Earliest Israel is essentially misguided. Such a quest, it is urged, involves a misuse of narrative texts which are far too late in origin, circa ninth century BCE at the earliest (but most of them considerably later), to be generally trustworthy carriers of historical memory over nearly half a millennium gap in direct evidence. 'History can only be described on the basis of literary traditions which record events and specify persons and places' (Noth 1960; 42).

If, on the other hand, 'history' is more simply and accurately defined as the totality of human experience, most of human history is ruled out as indescribable on the strictly documentary approach. On such a view archaeological evidence is important but mostly neutral, because it is overwhelmingly mute.

Here it will be better to withhold judgment on the extent to which artifacts 'speak', until we have reviewed again what archaeologists have found in the Transjordan. The question of 'what archaeology can and cannot do', as the mentor of most practitioners now arguing the matter made clear (Wright 1971; 1982), will be conditioned in no small way by the archaeologist's range of interests.

Chapter 1

TRANSITIONS IN OLD TRANSJORDAN

The Farmer and the Shepherd are Brothers

A touchstone of all recent attempts to reconstruct the history of the early biblical community in Transjordan was the pioneering surface-survey work of Nelson Glueck. Between 1932 and 1947 Glueck's fieldwork was almost entirely devoted to exploration of the Transjordan plateau and the Arabah-rift as far as Aqaba (Glueck 1934; 1935; 1939; 1949). Travelling mostly on foot or on horseback, Glueck sought out ancient ruins and collected artifacts, especially potsherds. He concluded that, after a period of strong Bronze Age civilization in the north (from the Yarmuq to, roughly, the Zarqa [biblical Jabboq]), and on the 'Moabite' plateau between the Wadi Mujib (biblical Arnon) and the Wadi Hasa (biblical Zered), from the twenty-third to eighteenth centuries BCE, there was a nearly complete gap in sedentary occupation and widescale reversion to nomadism. But the gap closed rapidly with the emergence of the Kingdom of Moab, c. mid-thirteenth century BCE. Glueck's conclusions were reinforced by de Vaux's explorations in the Beqa' and the area south of the Zarqa centering in es-Salt (de Vaux 1938).

Today, Glueck's 'gap hypothesis' is in serious need of further updating, such as Glueck himself began to provide in a provisional way (Glueck 1970; 140-41). It is worth noting that as recently as 1977 a very good thesis written at the University of Jordan, on the subject of 'Late Bronze Age Pottery in Jordan (East Bank)', concluded that available data did not compel a major revision of Glueck's theory (Kafafi 1977). I continue to be puzzled by the vigor and tone of Glueck's posthumous opposition.

It is now clear that the Transjordan plateau was far from being devoid of sedentary population in the Middle Bronze II period, which ended in widespread political and economic turmoil. Yet, as will become clear in the following pages, there is no evidence for a significant influx of nomads from the desert fringe, nor of widescale reversion to pastoral nomadism, at the transition from Middle Bronze to Late Bronze in Transjordan, but something of the reverse. While the evidence from excavations and surveys suggests a slight increase in density of sedentary population, from the Yarmuq to the Mujib after the Middle Bronze II period, the number of settlements south of the Mujib increases sharply in Late Bronze.

Unfortunately the surveys of periods represented by ceramic cultures have rarely attended as closely as do prehistorians to evidence of campsites, left behind by folk who used little or no pottery; and so we have very little 'hard data' on the tent-dwellers of old Transjordan.

Meanwhile, however, insights from anthropologists and the social sciences have led to more sophisticated questions. The 'Nomads' of any period are not directly represented in the survey results, unless, of course, they are related to one or another village group. In fact that is frequently the case, with farming and shepherding being specialized functions within a single lineage. There is now a sizable literature on the 'di-morphic' society (Rowton 1973a; 1973b; 1974; 1976a; 1976b; 1976c; 1977; Matthews 1978; Galvin 1981; Redding 1981).

Whether the referent be ancient or modern, the terms 'sedenterization' and 'nomadization' stand for poles of a societal continuum, with many possible degrees of interdependence and reciprocal influence, and with more than a few factors involved in a trend away from one subsistence strategy to the other. It is a two-way street. Especially along the desert fringe, a shift in the line of minimum rainfall necessary for dry-farming, a few kilometers one way or the other for only a few years in succession, could mean boom or bust for the agriculturalists. In the case of the former, the increasing needs of expanding urban centers for more agricultural surplus often leads to a redirection of the farmers' capital into more lucrative crops (especially vineyards, oliveyards, orchards), in the generally higher rainfall areas. Thus a combination of disproportionate redirection of capital by farmers, and a corresponding decrease in dry-farming, plus increasing extortionists demands of an expanding urban elite as the system becomes overloaded, encourages flight to the fringes, that is, reversion to transhumant pastoralism, the hardiest of all subsistence strategies.

It is well established that such reversion to transhumant pastoralism in Transjordan, since about the fifteenth century BCE, has been greatest in three periods, each following the imposition of imperial rule from a distant base: from Persia and Syria (6th to 2nd centuries BCE), from Baghdad and Egypt (8th to 10th centuries CE), and from Istanbul (16th to early 20th centuries CE). That factors other than merely foreign rule are involved is clear from the Roman and Byzantine periods, when the density and distribution of sedentary population in the Transjordan rose to an all-time high, unmatched again until mid-twentieth century CE.

This description is admittedly macrocosmic. We are still a long way from having the information to write a social and economic history of any one district in the Transjordan, comparable to L. Marfoe's work on the Lebanese Beqa‘ valley (Marfoe 1979), D.C. Hopkins on the Cisjordan hill country (Hopkins 1985), or L.E. Stager on the village family (Stager 1985b). Two surveys which entered the field in 1983-84 hold promise of filling some major gaps: the Irbid/Beit Ras Project in the north (Lenzen and McQuitty 1983), and the Madaba Plains Project in the near south of Amman (Geraty et al., 1986). Both projects aim to get at the problems involved in discerning and understanding the shifting patterns of subsistence strategies, in their socio-political nexus, for limited regions, that is, the catchment areas for two major ancient towns.

Proliferation of Archaeological Surveys

It would be difficult to exaggerate the pace of archaeological activity in Jordan in the years since Glueck's explorations, and especially the last decade. In 1973 the Department of Antiquities of Jordan published a set of maps and site lists, with brief introductions to each period, *The Archaeological Heritage of Jordan* (Barakat 1973).

Early Bronze 63 sites (including 5 west bank)
Middle Bronze 26 sites (including 2 west bank)
Late Bronze 14 sites (including 3 west bank)
Iron Age 145 sites (including 4 west bank)

Figure 1. Summary based on *The Archaeological Heritage of Jordan* (1973).

While no explanation of what qualified for inclusion as a 'site' is provided in the volume, the distributions and relative density of settlements throughout the pre-Hellenistic periods, as summarized only a decade ago, are instructive when compared to the present situation.

A number of archaeological survey teams working in Jordan in recent years have added a myriad of sites. Three of the more ambitious surveys have been reported in enough detail to afford reliable comparison and to contribute, cautiously, to a new synthesis. It is a truism that surface surveys, without stratigraphic excavations, may be misleading, especially in large sites with continuous or repeated occupation over hundreds of years. While the top and slopes of a mound will show a heavy distribution of sherds from the last main period of occupation, even centuries of erosion on the slopes may not suffice to expose deeper levels which will be poorly represented, or entirely missing, at the pottery reading. The vast majority of sites now known, however, are not large mounds. In these pages a 'site' is any place where investigators have reported clustered evidence of ancient handiwork that is datable, chiefly potsherds. The continued refinement of the pottery chronology for Transjordan, over the past two decades has happily sharpened awareness of some remaining, 'unrefined', gaps.

Given these reminders about the state of the art, we may proceed with some confidence to collate results of the survey teams recently at work in Jordan. The sample of sites is surely large enough to offset misreadings of potsherds here and there, and to allay suspicions about gaps large enough to skew seriously the general archaeological picture.

The first extensive survey in the years since Glueck, covering 346 sites in northern Jordan between the Yarmuq and the Zarqa (biblical Jabboq) rivers, was published by S. Mittmann, but without including pottery photos, drawings, or descriptions (Mittmann 1970). P.W. Lapp, B. Hennessey, and P. Mortensen helped Mittmann read the pottery.

The Survey of Central and Southern Moab, which spent three seasons in the field (1978, 1979, 1982), headed by J.M. Miller, recorded 585 sites. Results have been reported briefly in journal articles by various members of the team (Miller 1979a; 1979b; Mattingly 1983; Kautz 1981). My thanks to Gerald Mattingly for sharing a printout of the Late Bronze pottery sites.

The East Jordan Valley Survey, sponsored jointly by the Department of Antiquities of Jordan (M. Ibrahim), the American Center of Oriental Research (J. Sauer), and Jordan University (K. Yassine),

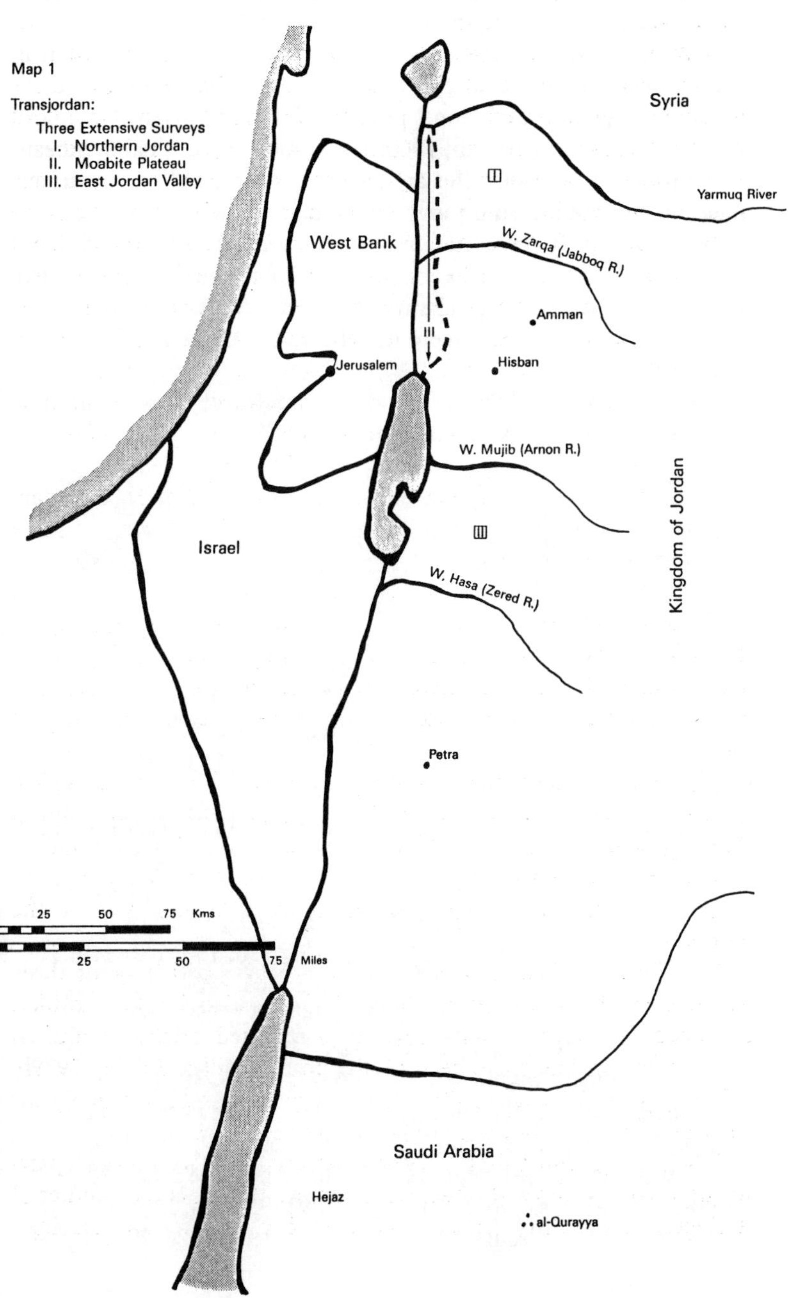

Map 1
Transjordan:
Three Extensive Surveys
I. Northern Jordan
II. Moabite Plateau
III. East Jordan Valley
Syria
Yarmuq River
West Bank
W. Zarqa (Jabboq R.)
Amman
III
Hisban
Jerusalem
W. Mujib (Arnon R.)
Israel
W. Hasa (Zered R.)
Kingdom of Jordan
Petra
25
50
75
Kms
25
50
75
Miles
Saudi Arabia
Hejaz
al-Qurayya

spent two seasons in the field beginning in 1975. The survey area extends from the Yarmuq to the Dead Sea and from the Jordan River eastwards to the first rise of foothills. Extensive excavations had already been conducted at two major sites with abundant evidence for the Late Bronze and Iron I periods: Tell es-Sa'idiyeh (Pritchard 1964a; 1964b; 1965a; 1965b; 1966; 1980); and Tabaqat Fahl, ancient Pella (Smith 1973). Both sites are within the upper half of the survey area, between the Yarmuq and Wadi Rajib, which was covered in 1975 and promptly reported (Ibrahim, Sauer, and Yassine: 1976). In that first season 106 sites were recorded, of which 54 were known from previous archaeological surveys (chiefly Mellaart 1962 and de Contenson 1964); 52 sites were new additions to the archaeological map.

The data, for our periods, from these three surveys, as reported in various publications, is tabulated in Figure 2.

Total Sites	*Mb II*	*LB*	*Iron I*	*LB Iron I*
North Jordan	346 21[a]6.1%)	23[b]6.6%)	77[c](22%)	19(5.5%)
Moab	585 31?(5.3%)	275(12.8%)	---	---
Jordan Valley, N	106 25[d](23.6%)	13[e](12.3%)	23[f](21.7%)	8(7.5%)

Figure 2. Three major archaeological surveys.

a. Mittmann, sites 15, 23, 31, 33?, 39, 58, 77?, 103, 108, 191, 196, 206, 213, 228, 246, 297, 316, 325, 333, 337, 338, 340, 341. This leaves out 9 sites plotted on the line between MB and LB, which I take to mean 'undifferentiated', or the like (75?, 101, 147, 168, 183, 204?, 240, 252, and 290).

b. Mittmann, sites 12, 14, 15, 18, 19, 24, 54, 58, 60, 70, 71, 81, 88?, 91, 101, 103, 185, 196, 210, 282, 311, 336, 337, 345.

c. Mittmann, sites 3, 7, 8, 10, 12, 14, 18, 19, 24, 31, 40?, 43?, 54, 58, 59, 61, 62, 63, 64, 65, 66, 70, 71, 81, 88?, 101, 103, 104, 115, 116, 128, 132, 133, 134, 138, 140, 141, 142, 147, 155, 156, 159, 161, 166, 168, 170, 182, 183, 185, 193, 194, 196, 198, 202, 203?, 204, 206, 207, 210, 211, 212, 215, 223, 227, 237, 238, 240, 247, 252, 259, 262, 282, 290, 295, 297, 307, 311, 325, 336, 337, 342?, 345.

d. Ibrahim, Sauer, Yassine; sites 13, 26, 27, 28, 29, 30, 33, 34, 40, 45, 47 poss. MB/LB, 56, 58 south site, 69, 78 main site poss., 79 poss., 81 1 poss., 84 prob., 85 few poss., 92, 95, 96 dom., 99, 100, 103.

e. Ibrahim, Sauer, Yassine; sites 6, 7, 26, 47 poss. MB/LB, 78 prob., 79 poss., 85, 87 poss., 89 LB/Iron I, 92, 93, 95 poss. IA, 103.

f. Ibrahim, Sauer, Yassine; sites 3 poss., 6, 7, 19 few, 26, 29 few poss.,

33, 34, 40 few poss., 61 Iron I dom., 65 few, 77, 78, 81 Iron IC dom., 82 few, 89 LB/Iron I, 92, 93 Iron IB, 94 Iron IB dom., 102, 103, 104, 105 few.

From Middle Bronze to Late Bronze

Out of a total of 346 sites examined between the Yarmuq and Zarqa Rivers, Mittmann reports MB II pottery at 21 sites (or 6.1% of all sites in his survey). Mittmann's pottery readings are conveniently presented in tabular form in the publication (1970: 256-64). I have not included here Mittmann's MB I sites, because of continuing debates about EB IV, a category which Mittmann does not use. Mittmann reports another 12 sites with sherds that are possibly MB II (3 sites) or on the line between MB and LB (9 sites), which might raise the number of sites in one or both categories if the readings were clear.

Turning to 'Moab', we are told that '31 sites yielded sherds that are definitely Middle Bronze . . ., each site having between 1 and 46 sherds with this designation' (Mattingly 1983: 256). According to the same essay, two sites have sherds that are definitely MB I. Do the same two sites also show MB II? Or should the figure for the latter be 29? In neither case would it seriously affect results for comparison with MB II in the north.

These two surveys show that there was a *distribution* of sedentary population in MB II 'Moab' which compares very favorably (c. 5.3% of all sites reported) with the situation in the north (6.1% of all sites in Mittmann's survey). A major difference in MB is the number of walled towns in the north (compared with a total absence of such sites on the 'Moab' plateau), thanks mainly, we may suppose, to the richer agricultural conditions in the Jordan Valley and upper reaches of major wadi systems, especially the Yarmuq. Here there developed much earlier a tradition of city-state polity, as reflected in both biblical and extrabiblical sources.

In contrast to both northern Jordan and the plateau south of Wadi Mujib, the upper Jordan Valley had a far higher density and distribution of sedentary population in MB II (25 sites; 23.6% of all sites in the survey area). The contrast is striking indeed. In view of the fact that the goals and methods of the two later surveys were closely comparable and achieved more intensive coverage, while both were heirs to improved stratigraphic controls for pottery chronology, it is the earlier work in northern Jordan that most needs to be updated. The Irbid/Beit Ras Project, excavating in 1984, added Irbid to the list of 'definite' MB II sites, also fortified (Lenzen and McQuitty: private communication). The figures for both MB II and LB in northern Jordan will no doubt be revised upward, as additional returns are reported, but probably not enough to offset very much the comparison with the upper Jordan Valley in MB.

Turning now to Late Bronze, two points of contrast stand out. First, the lower density of sedentary occupation in northern Jordan from MB II (6.1% of all sites surveyed by Mittmann) continues at about the same level into LB (6.6%). But only four of the twenty-one sites with MB II pottery also produced LB I readings (Mittmann, sites 15, 58, 196, and 337)! In other words *the transition from MB to LB in northern Jordan brought a slight increase in the number of settlements, and the settlements are drastically redistributed.*

The increase in number of LB settlements appears to be slightly greater as one moves south. Surveys were carried out in preparation for development of three major reservoirs: the Maqarin Dam on the Yarmuq, a Wadi Arab reservoir, and the King Talal Dam on the Zarqa. The report distinguishes between large 'areas', defined after general reconnaissance, and 'sites'. The latter were 'distinguished by the concentration of artifacts . . . and/or architectural remains' (Kerestes et al. 1978: 110). Results gleaned from the publication may be tabulated, for our periods, as follows in Figure 3.

Maqarin Dam	*13 areas*	*31 sites*
Late Bronze	0 (sic!)	2
Iron Age	2	2
Wadi Arab	*2 areas*	*3 sites*
Late Bronze	0	0
Iron Age	1	1
King Taal Dam	*6 areas*	*14 sites*
Late Bronze	1	2
Iron Age	0	3

Figure 3. Late Bronze and Iron Age: Dam Reservoirs

On the plateau to the east and south of W. Arab, the Irbid/Beit Ras Project, begun in 1983, added three more sites to the LB list in 1984 (Irbid, Kufr Yuba, and Ham). The team conducted salvage excavations at Irbid, where they uncovered a heavy burn layer late in LB followed by Iron I occupation (Lenzen and McQuitty, private communication, confirmed on our visit to the site). They also report LB pottery from Tell Sal (outside the project area).

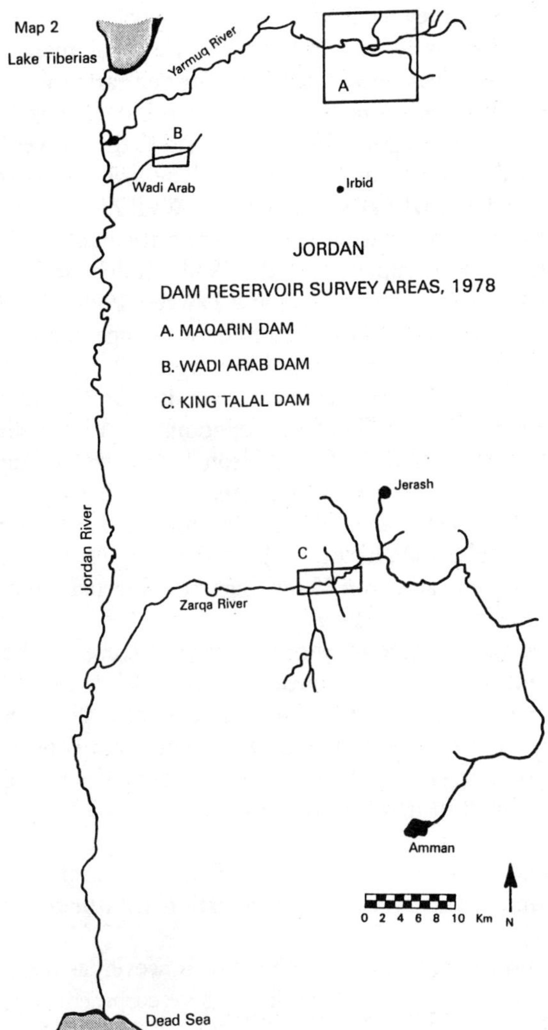
Map 2
Lake Tiberias
Yarmuq River
A
B
Wadi Arab
Irbid
JORDAN
DAM RESERVOIR SURVEY AREAS, 1978
A. MAQARIN DAM
B. WADI ARAB DAM
C. KING TALAL DAM
Jerash
C
Jordan River
Zarqa River
Amman
0 2 4 6 8 10 Km
N
Dead Sea

At the same time, a modified 'gap hypothesis' seems to be faring well in the Wadi Ziqlab (as in the lower Zarqa basin, see below). In the Wadi Ziqlab the survey team adopted a strategy of random sampling, plotting the survey area into 115 squares, 1 × 1 kilometer. From a 20% sample of squares, good diagnostics for our earlier periods were generally lacking; therefore 'Middle Bronze-Late Bronze' became one category in the report. Two of the 'sites' thus covered could possibly be MB-LB forts or watchtowers. The low density of sherds most often read as 'MB-LB' suggests to the Wadi Ziqlab survey team small camps more than permanent farming settlements. 'It is during the Iron Age that occupation of the Wadi Ziqlab drainage basin became well established' (Banning and Fawcett 1983: 300-301).

The pattern is similar at the eastern desert fringe of north-central Transjordan. In the report of pottery from 48 locations in the Hawran and eastern Jordanian desert 'there is sporadic indication of Early, Middle, and Late Bronze occupation. . . . A very slight, but nonetheless persistent indication of Iron I and Iron II appears at certain sites in the area' (King, Lenzen, and Rollefson 1983: 430). Even 'sporadic' may be an overstatement for MB/LB (1 body sherd at Site 8, Umm al-Surab: location V) and for Iron I (4 sherds [3 bods] at Site 16, Hawshiyan). Iron II readings are reported, however, for twelve locations.

Returning to the three extensive surveys (Figure 2), the second point of contrast is on the plateau south of Wadi Mujib. There, comparison with the north, based on admittedly sketchy preliminary publications, shows a percentage of sites with Late Bronze pottery (12.8%) more than twice as high as the preceding MB II in the same region (5.3%) and nearly double the percentage of LB in the north (6.6%). In addition, Miller's team reports that another '47 sites yielded sherds that are *possibly* Late Bronze . . . each site having between 1 and 37 sherds with this designation' (Mattingly 1983: 256, italics mine).

This picture appears to change abruptly, however, as we move into the deep wadis dropping abruptly from the escarpment to the Dead Sea, judging from the intensive survey of Wadi 'Isal, circa 7 kilometers south of Kerak. This survey covered both sides of the wadi flanking the old Roman road, in 50 m. strips, recording 90 sites, mostly 'transient occupations at best', with no clear signs of settlements prior to Iron II. But the latter shows up at 24 sites (Jacobs 1983).

A team from the German Institute in Amman, working out of Kerak in 1984, added one more isolated Late Bronze settlement to the map (A. Knauf, private communication).

On the southeastern plain of the Dead Sea, after the demise of the Early Bronze towns, there is a long gap in ceramic evidence until Iron I and especially Iron II (Rast and Schaub 1974; also see McCreery 1978).

The survey results for Iron I in Moab have not yet been announced. The picture that is presented above, however, indicates that the plateau between Wadi Mujib and Wadi Hasa saw a significant explosion of sedentary population in the Late Bronze Age, in contrast to both the far north, and as we shall see below, the near south (Edom). The expanded sedentary population was not all locally begotten. Nor could much of it have come from the desert.

Comparison with the upper half of the Jordan Valley is equally instructive. While the number of settlements declined by half in the transition from MB (23.6% of all sites) to LB (12.3%), the distribution of sedentary population on the 'Moabite' plateau appears to have more than doubled (up from 5.3% in MB to 12.8% in LB)!

Recent excavations in the Jordan Valley continue to sharpen the picture. Tell Mazar shows both periods (Yassine 1984). Kataret es-Samra has LB I and II (Leonard 1979; 1981); and continuing work at Pella in 1984 turned up a Late Bronze destruction layer (private communication).

Early Iron Age

Turning at last to the beginning of the Iron Age (see Figure 2), one observation is clearly in order, while awaiting further returns. Despite the sharp increase in sedentary occupation in northern Jordan (22% of all Mittmann's sites show Iron I), the transition to Iron I was far more peaceful there than at the end of Middle Bronze, where, as noted above, only four of the twenty-one MB II sites also produced LB I sherds. At the end of LB in northern Jordan it is just the reverse: of the twenty-three LB sites, nineteen continue producing potsherds into Iron I.

Similarly in the upper Jordan Valley, after a drastic reduction in number of sites (from 25 in MB II to 13 in LB), eight of the latter continued to be occupied as the figure climbs back in Iron I to about what it had been in MB (23 sites).

The conclusion is inescapable that the first half of the Late Bronze period was an especially turbulent one in the Jordan Valley, as has long been known to be true for Cisjordan (see below). The prolonged turbulence must have precipitated large scale emigration out of the valley and points further west, and up onto the Transjordan plateau where there were fewer fortified cities and none south of the Mujib. It was there that the first of the large territorial states in Transjordan would emerge, in the thirteenth century, as the 'kingdom' of Moab.

Excursus on Cisjordan

For comparison with patterns west of the Jordan River we now have an excellent study, 'Urban Canaan in the Late Bronze Age', by R. Gonen (1984), based on the data for continuity of settlement, from the MB II period to the thirteenth century BCE, at 77 excavated sites. The list of 77 includes only sites that were either reoccupied in some phase of the Late Bronze period, or though abandoned, had nearby Late Bronze Age cemeteries. The sites in the control sample are classified by Gonen, according to size:

1. Up to 10 dunams (4 dunams = 1 acre) = tiny settlements.
2. 11 to 50 dunams = small settlements.
3. 51 to 100 dunams = medium-sized settlements.
4. 101-199 dunams = large settlements.
5. 200 + dunams = very large settlements.

Of the 77 sites in the control sample, only 17 were occupied without interruption from the Middle Bronze period into the Late Bronze period. The number of settlements, represented by the 77 sites, are phased as follows:

MB II	54 (minimum)
16th century	24
15th century	28
14th century	48
13th century	56

As was shown above, for the upper Jordan Valley, the decrease in number of settlements is drastic in the transition from the Middle Bronze period into the first half of the Late Bronze period. After that, however, 'town life picked up in the 14th century BC, and by the 13th century the number of occupied sites climbed back to Middle Bronze levels' (Gonen 1984: 62).

Gonen next brings into the picture the information from surface surveys; the contrast between Middle and Late Bronze periods is even sharper. The number of Late Bronze settlements in the regions surveyed adds up to only 37 percent of the total for the Middle Bronze period. Gonen is aware that a certain margin of error must be allowed (given the problematics of surface data), and offers two observations. First, the Late Bronze period settlements were greatly reduced in size, most often unwalled, with many of them concentrated on the acropoli of tells. Second, 'there was a shift of settlement concentration to the coastal plain and along important communication routes. The mountainous parts of the country and the inner regions, where most surveys have been conducted, certainly suffered from a process of desertion' (Gonen 1984: 66).

Study of settlement size in Cisjordan is especially instructive, as represented by Figure 4.

Number of Settlements from MB II to 13th century
(by size groups, percents)

Site size	MBII	16th cent.	15th cent.	14th cent.	13th cent.
1	11	29	37	37	43
2 + 3	61	59	52	58	52
4 + 5	28	12	12	5	5

Figure 4. Cisjordan settlements grouped by period and size (Gonen 1984: 66, Table 3).

While the percentage of small and medium-sized settlements (size 2 and 3) remained rather constant throughout all phases, the number of tiny settlements increased fourfold by the end of Late Bronze (up from 11% to 43%). At the same time, the number of large and very large settlements is sharply reduced. In fact, of the six sites in Class 5, only Lachish and Hazor survived for the duration of the Late Bronze period.

Finally, Gonen compares actual size of all settlements, in the control sample, for which information is available. The results, again, are startling:

> Even in the 13th century BC, when the number of settlements was nearly comparable to that of the MB II period, the total occupied area was only about 45 percent of the listed area of MB II period settlements, which actually means that it was much less. It is also apparent that the gradual increase in number of settlements between the 16th and 13th centuries added only about 12 percent to the occupied area (Gonen 1984: 68).

All this reflects 'a breakdown of the system of medium to large city-states that formed the backbone of Middle Bronze Age Canaan' (Gonen 1984: 69). The breakdown meant an escalating cycle of inter-city warfare and its sequel in plagues and famines, leaving in its wake a much reduced population.

Gonen is especially impressed by the nearly total lack of defense walls around the Late Bronze period settlements. She suggests that it may be an outcome of Egyptian policy in Canaan, intended to weaken the power of the semi-autonomous city-states (Gonen 1984: 70). If so, it was a policy that only paved the way for a sudden flowering of new farming settlements in the hill country at the beginning of the Iron Age (Stager 1976), which in turn represented the move to total independence of a 'tribal league', that is, Early Israel.

Edom and the Deep South

Returning to the scene in Transjordan, archaeology is still a long way from having sufficient data from excavated sites. And there are much larger areas still awaiting intensive survey. The problem is especially acute in the territory of ancient Edom.

South of the Moab plateau and the Wadi el-Hasa, the situation at the end of Late Bronze and early in Iron I appears quite different, but not unrelated to the burgeoning population on the plateau just to the north in the same period. On the basis of her excavations at Umm el-Biyarah, Tawilan, and Buseirah (probably Bozrah, erstwhile capital city of Edom), C. Bennett has made some sweeping claims about biblical tradition on the area. All three sites lack Iron I pottery. The earliest at Umm el-Biyarah is seventh century, the earliest at Tawilan ninth century, and the earliest at Bozrah possibly tenth century. Bennett finds no evidence in her excavations for a territorial 'kingdom' of Edom until well into the period of Iron II. Thus the biblical tradition on early Edom 'probably reflects 8th-6th century BC conditions' (Bennett 1983: 16). Much turns here upon an assumption regarding what range of polities may be embraced under 'kingdom', a question to which we shall return at the end of this section.

The Wadi el-Hasa Archaeological Survey (WHS) spent three seasons in the field, between 1979 and 1982 (MacDonald, Banning, and Paulish 1980; MacDonald, Rollefson, and Roller 1982; MacDonald, et al. 1983). The project area was the south bank of Wadi el-Hasa (biblical Zered River) and tributaries, including only the northern portion of ancient 'Edom'. It was an intensive survey which overlaps only in part the extensive exploration of N. Glueck. The goals of the survey included also a search for prehistoric sites (generally beyond the purview of the Moab and north Jordan surveys, but not the Jordan Valley team of Ibrahim, Sauer, and Yassine). The result is a list of over 1000 sites from the south bank of the Wadi el-Hasa. At this writing I can do no more than to quote from some pre-publication pages graciously supplied by the director of the WHS team, Burton MacDonald.

> There was no definite Middle Bronze period pottery collected in the survey area. Fifteen Middle-Bronze - Late-Bronze Age sherds were collected at Site 64 . . . . Late Bronze sherds were not found except in relation to Iron Ages sites. Four body sherds were collected from Site 172 . . . read as either Middle Bronze, Late Bronze, or Iron Age. This is a predominantly Byzantine site . . . . Late Bronze period sites . . . are almost non-existent in the survey area. However there were five sites at which Late-Bronze—Iron-Age period sherds were collected. All these sites are located in the western extremity of the survey area:
>
> Site 178 Ras Rihab
> Site 168 now a cemetery, S. Bank of Wadi Hasa
> Site 106 in Wadi eth-Thamad
> Site 145 Kh. Ain el-Ghuzlan
> Site 147 Ash-Shorabat
>
> (MacDonald, private communication, summer 1984).

Thus there appears to have been a series of small, but permanent, settlements along the south bank of Wadi el-Hasa by the early twelfth century (MacDonald et al. 1982: 126-27; 1983: 5-8; MacDonald 1984: 117). Elsewhere MacDonald has written

> there is a very strong case for Glueck's position that the area south of Wadi el-Hasa was occupied between the 13th-12th centuries BC. However, we differ in details as to where that Iron Age occupation was located (MacDonald 1983b: 20).

In a separate article devoted to a series of sites explained as 'Edomite Border Fortresses' by Glueck, MacDonald reports negative conclusions, even for an Iron II date, if the sites were related as part of a system. 'However, there are other possibilities for an Iron Age II fortress system along the south bank of the Wadi which require further investigation' (MacDonald 1984: 121).

Somewhat further south and east, the Archaeological and Epigraphic

Survey of the Aqaba-Ma'an area has reported clear Iron I readings for two sites (out of a total of fifteen), both in the Wadi Rumman: Rakbat Umm Edgeyer and Jebel Utud (Jobling 1981: 110). At Tell el-Kharaz (G.R. 194911), one of seven sites covered in 1982, soundings by C. Bennett show occupation from the Pottery Neolithic to the end of Middle Bronze, while surface sherding suggests re-occupation 'during the Iron Age' (Jobling 1983: 189).

While awaiting further returns from 'Edom', we can say that the beginning of early Iron Age settlements along the south bank of Wadi el-Hasa looks like spillover from a burgeoning population on the plateau to the north. The formation of a sizable territorial state, 'Kingdom' of Edom, would thus lag considerably behind its northern neighbor. But the kings who ruled from Bozrah in the eighth century and later very likely had lesser and local predecessors, often themselves contemporaries, each one claiming the clout that went with being 'king' (cf. use of the *mlk* title among the pastoralists known from Mari some 500 years earlier, and the 'kings' of Midian who appear as contemporaries of early Israel). One of the predecessors may well have been 'the Edomite king' who opposed advance of Israel, in the wilderness traditions (Num. 20.18), while another one, possibly more or less contemporary, in another traditionary strand, did not (if that is the implication of Deut. 2.4-8). Who can say? Certainly, on present evidence, neither the archaeologist nor the literary critic. Better to leave it an open question.

Northern Hejaz and 'Midianite' Pottery

Immediately to the south of Edom was the heartland of ancient Midian, in the northern Hejaz of Saudi Arabia. It has become clear from recent survey work, that the northern Hejaz and Tabuk regions 'begin to be intensively settled during the late second millennium' BCE (Ingraham et al. 1981: 71). A distinctive painted pottery now long known to be widely but lightly dispersed through southern to central Transjordan, found as well on both sides of the Arabah and in the southern Negeb, is generally dubbed 'Midianite' and confidently dated to the last centuries of the Late Bronze period. The pottery is known in considerable abundance from two sites in the Hejaz (Tayma and Qurayya) and one in the southern Negeb (Timna). Qurayya (Map 1), where the pottery predominates as 'local and common' (Parr et al. 1970), lies seventy kilometers north of Tabuk, a little more than sixty kilometers from the Jordanian frontier at Mudawwara. Qurayya is in fact a very good candidate for the place name (Beth-) Yahweh, found in Egyptian topographical lists from the reigns of Amenophis III (1417-1379 BCE) and Ramesses II (1304-1237 BCE); see Cross (1973: 61-62) and Giveon (1964: 239-55, especially 244).

The pottery of Qurayya shows several distinctive traits, both in structure and decoration, so that it is distinguishable from Iron Age 'Edomite' painted wares. Paste ranges from cream to red, commonly with coarse temper. Most pieces are wheel made. While there are some bichrome patterns, most decoration is polychrome (red, black, brown, yellow) on a cream slip. Birds and animals are common motifs, but geometric features also are found (Parr et al. 1970: 238). 'A predominantly Egyptian inspiration for the Midianite ware' is most attractive (Parr 1982: 130).

Outside the northwestern corner of Saudi Arabia this pottery is best known from the Late Bronze period Hathor Temple at Timna north of Elat, which the excavator thinks became a tented 'Midianite' shrine in its later phase (Rothenberg 1972: 184). Some 'Midianite' sherds were previously found at nearby Kheleifeh (Glueck 1967) and various other sites in the eastern Arabah (Glueck 1935) and, later, on the Coral Island (Jezirat Faroun) south of Elat (Rothenberg 1972: 204). Still other sites had produced scattered specimens (Parr et al. 1970: 239). More recently, examples of this pottery have turned up at sites in Israel: Tell Masos (Aharoni et al. 1975: 109), Tell Jdur (Ben-Arieh 1978: 60-61), and Yotvata (Meshel 1975a: 49-50; 1975b: 50-51; Kalsbeek and London 1978). A few sherds are reported found in Transjordan at Tawilan (Parr et al. 1970: 38-39), Um Guwe'ah (Jobling 1981: 110), and the Amman citadel (Kalsbeek and London 1978).

The 1980 survey of the Northwestern Province of Saudi Arabia collected Qurayya-type pottery at fourteen sites, thirteen of which are located in the coastal wadis of the northern Hejaz (Ingraham et al. 1980: 59). A two-day reconnaissance of Qurayya confirmed the existence of a complex irrigation network for climax farming at Qurayya, from very early times (Parr et al. 1970: 240-41; Ingraham et al. 1981: 72). The presence of Qurayya-type pottery previously noted at Tayma and Mugha'ir Shuy'ab (Parr et al. 1970: 240) was amply confirmed (Ingraham et al. 1981: 74).

Returning, for a moment, to southern Jordan, the Wadi el-Hasa survey has yet to find any clearly recognizable 'Midianite' pottery. Not a scrap (MacDonald, private communication, summer, 1984). Even more surprising, in view of the Late Bronze dates for Timna, are the returns from the rich copper mining district in the Wadi Feinan, which was certainly worked in the Iron Age (Bachmann and Hauptmann 1984). After another season in the field, the German team had still to find a single 'Midianite' sherd (private communication, November 1984). 'Thus the northern presence of Midianite pottery seems', largely, 'confined to the areas of the Arabah, Negev, and Sinai' contiguous with the distribution in Northwestern Saudi Arabia (Bawden 1983: 39). Distribution and frequencies do indeed point to the northern Hejaz as the homeland of the 'Midianite' pottery-makers (Parr et al. 1970: 24; Rothenberg 1972: 182; Bawden 1983: 39).

The flourishing sedentary occupation in the coastal wadis of the northern Hejaz at the close of the Late Bronze period presents a sharp contrast to the situation in the contemporary 'Edomite' territory just to the north and the still unsettled stretches of Arabia to the south. Qurayya and Tayma controlled principle trade routes. It was W.F. Albright who assembled the evidence and mustered arguments for a wide-ranging Midianite monopoly of the donkey-caravaneering desert trade (Albright 1970). More recently it has been argued that the non-Semitic names of several Midianite 'kings' (Evi, Reqem, and Reba in Num. 31.8), as well as the place name Madon (= Midian?) in Galilee (Josh. 11.1) may well be Anatolian in origin (Mendenhall 1973: 167-68). It is likely, Mendenhall also suggests, that a second wave of immigration from the north brought the domesticated camel, which would make the Midianites of the Judges era such effective tax collectors in the days of Gideon (Judges 6-8).

In other words, the emergence of a Midianite state, possibly a pentapolis of locally prominent 'kings', by the late thirteenth century BCE, may be understood as part of the same vast disruptions at the breakup of the Hittite empire, which brought 'Sea Peoples' to Egypt and the coasts of Syria-Palestine, and giving rise to at least two Amorite regimes (Sihon and Og) in the power vacuum that had previously existed north and south of the Jabboq.

Amman and Vicinity

In the area between the Wadi ez-Zarqa and the Wadi Mujib, a number of regional surveys and recent excavations have filled many gaps, although there remain very large areas about which little is known in detail.

Excavations at the Amman Citadel (see Ward 1966); Bennett 1979; now especially Dornemann 1983) and the nearby Jebel Nuzha tomb (Dajani 1966) produced considerable evidence for our periods, especially the tomb (Ward 1966). The Late Bronze period 'Temple' uncovered at the Marqa Airport must have served a sedentary population, contrary to my earlier view (Boling 1969; 1975b); on the function of the building see L. Herr 1976 and 1986). It is now suggested, by B. Hennessy, the next to last excavator of the site, that the related settlement is to be found under the airport control tower (see Aharoni 1979: 277-78, n. 54).

Similarly, burial caves in the Baq'ah valley, where 19 out of a total of 33 examined in 1978 'dated to various phases of the Late Bronze Age' (McGovern 1981: 127; and 1982a) reflect a continuing sedentary occupation. The caves are now part of an established sequence: LB I in Cave A2, LB II/Iron Ia in Cave B3, and Iron Ia in Cave A4 (McGovern 1982b: 122-23; and 1982c). Settlements related to the same burial caves (McGovern 1980) have been partially excavated, at Rujm el-Henu with plan similar to the Marqa Airport building (McGovern 1983), and at Kh. Umm ad-Dananir (LB and Iron Ia), the latter appearing to be a walled settlement of approximately 2½ hectares (McGovern 1981, 1982).

Late Bronze period defense walls are found at Sahab, southeast of Amman, excavated by M. Ibrahim (1972, 1974, 1975), after discovery of an LB/Iron Age tomb at Sahab (Dajani 1970). At the southern edge of the Baq'ah Valley, Tell Safut has a Middle Bronze/Late Bronze defense system (see provisionally Ma'ayeh 1960: 4-5).

Finally, a series of mostly 'megalithic' structures, which ringed the site of ancient Rabbat Ammon, and which Glueck assigned to the early Iron Age, have been widely interpreted following Glueck as part of a planned defense system for the early Kingdom of Ammon (Glueck 1939; Gese 1958; Fohrer 1961; Reventlow 1963; Hentschke 1977; von Rabenau 1978), and a very successful system (Landes 1964). More recently, reservations based on improved pottery chronology and the absence of controlled excavations at most of the sites have been reinforced by results from three of the 'towers' that have been well dug and reported. The large round tower Rujm al-Malfuf North produced Roman sherds on bedrock (Boraas 1971). On the other hand, construction of a smaller round tower, Rujm al Malfuf South, is dated to the seventh to sixth centuries by the excavator. 'However, the Iron I material was in sufficient quantity to provide evidence for an Iron I presence in the area' (Thompson 1973). At Kh. al-Hajjar, walls and pottery on bedrock indicate that the site was first occupied and built up in Iron I (3 phases), after which there was apparently a 200 year gap in occupation, to the seven to sixth centuries BCE (Thompson 1972: 62; 1977: 34). I conclude that both the early origin for a number of these 'Ammonite towers' and the idea that they comprise a planned defense system remains an open question, increasingly losing ground to the burden of proof (Dornemann 1983: 123-24).

The Lower Zarqa

Despite the uncertainty about the towers, the situation described above, for the vicinity of Rabbat Ammon at the source of the Zarqa, and for the Baq'ah Valley adjacent on the north, nevertheless stands in sharp contrast to the lower Zarqa catchment area. From two seasons of intensive survey of Telul edh-Dhahab and a semicircular area of four to five kilometers radius to the east, south, and west (thus overlapping in part the explorations of de Vaux 1938), the preliminary report lists 32 sites. After a complete gap in evidence for Middle Bronze Age presence at any of the survey sites, one site only (Kh. Umm el-Idham) produced evidence for Late Bronze presence; and that was followed by occupation in the 'Early Iron Age'. At four other sites 'Early Iron' is *the main period* of occupation, with five additional sites showing evidence of occupation in the same period, and enough sherds to establish 'Early Iron' period presence at another four or five sites (Gordon and Villiers 1983).

From all of this we may reasonably conclude that an embryonic territorial state, 'Kingdom of Ammon', was in place at the edge of the desert, but not extending as far as the escarpment, by the end of the thirteenth century, in polar relationship to its larger southern contemporary 'Kingdom of Moab'. The latter, to judge from the biblical tradition, was soon to be found (if it was not already) seeking to expand north of the Mujib.

South of Amman

From the southern outskirts of Amman to the north bank of the Mujib, published materials from excavation and controlled tomb clearance are scarce, for the Late Bronze period and the transition to Iron I. See reports on el-Al (Weippert 1979: 26); Kh. el-Mekhayyat near Mount Nebo (Saller and Bagati 1949; cf. Dornemann 1983: 124, n. 1); a Madaba tomb (Harding 1953); Kh. al-Hajjar (Thompson 1972); Dhiban (Tushingham 1972); and Khirbet Ara'ir (Olivarri 1972: 77-94; 1976: 230-31 and Pl. I; cf. Dornemann 1983: 126).

Map 3 THE HESBAN REGION SURVEY

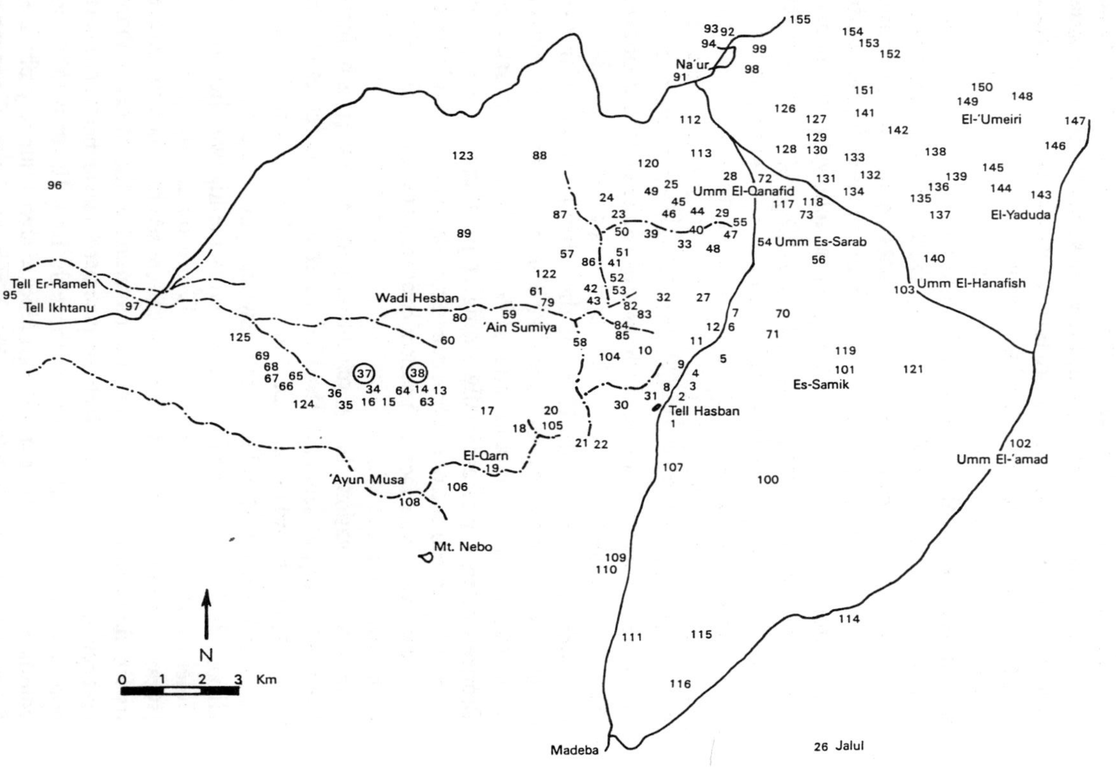

In this area the most substantial returns, for our periods, have come from the excavations of Tell Hesban and the associated regional survey (Map 3). Excavations established clearly that Hesban emerged as a flourishing town, at the earliest, late in Iron I (Boraas and Horn 1969; 1973; 1975; Boraas and Geraty 1976; 1978). What about its wider neighborhood? The Hesban Region Survey had its first goal 'to locate, within a ten-kilometer radius of Tell Hesban, all antiquities sites of the ceramic cultures, that is, from the pottery neolithic to the present' (Ibach 1981: 2). During three seasons in the field the Hesban Survey team collected data on 155 sites (the final publication will include 148 sites, the figure used here for tabulating comparisons), with results for our periods as follows in Figure 5.

Middle Bronze II	8 sites (5.5% of all sites)
Late Bronze	6 sites (4.1% " " ")
Iron I	30 sites (20% " " ")

Figure 5. Hesban Region Survey

Two of the six sites with 'LB' readings are dismissed as insignificant. 'Not only are the sites small but the LB sherds are few in number and questionable' (Ibach 1981: 125). Of the other four, #54 Umm es-Sarab is classified as 'medium-sized'. The other three are 'major' sites (#26 Jalul, #97 Iktanu, and #149 Tell el-Umeiri West). Late Bronze evidence was especially strong at Jalul and Umeiri (Ibach 1981: 127). In the entire Hesban Survey Area, only Jalul and Umeiri West show strong surface evidence of continuity from Middle Bronze II through Iron I.

In 1984 excavations began at Tell el-Umeiri West (the Madaba Plains Project), as sequel to the Hesban excavations. Tell el-Umeiri West (Maps 3 and 4, site 149) lies ten kilometers southeast of Amman's 'Seventh Circle', on the new highway to the international airport. It is the larger of two tells; across the highway lies Tell el-Umeiri East (Maps 3 and 4, site 150), predominantly Roman and Byzantine. The site of Umeiri West was chosen for study because of its location at the northern and opposite end of the Madaba Plains and because the surface indications promised a sequence very nearly continuous from Early Bronze through Iron II. It would thus complement the excellent stratigraphic sequence already obtained for the later periods from Tell Hesban. The first season of excavation showed existence of a Middle Bronze defense wall on the slope, but did not penetrate to Late Bronze or Iron I levels on top of the mound, for which there is considerable evidence in surface pottery.

Map 4

MADABA PLAINS PROJECT SURVEY 1984

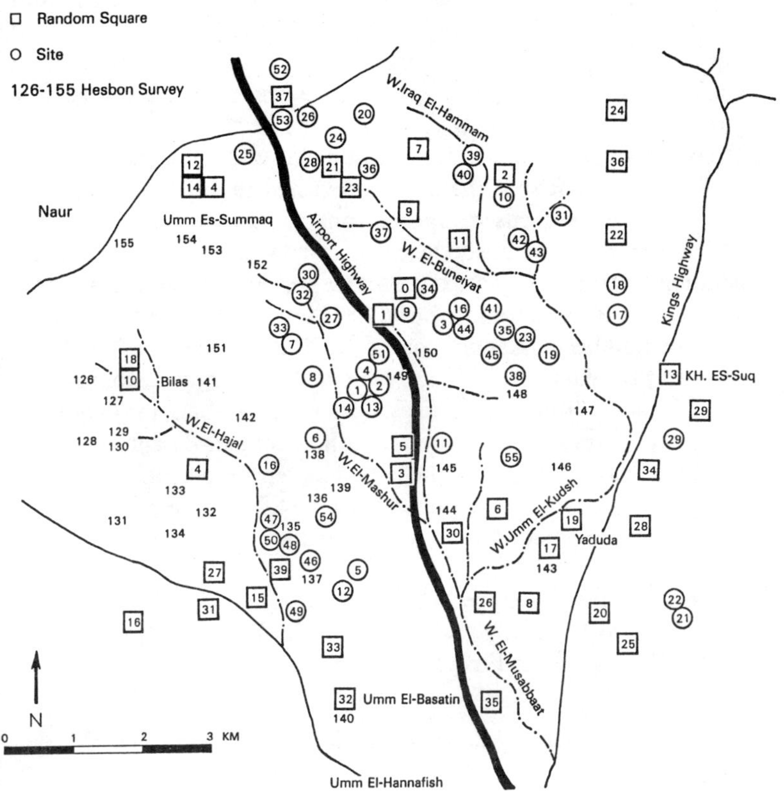

The Madaba Plains Regional Survey began at the same time, and I was privileged to participate as Field Archaeologist for the 1984 season. Thanks to the generosity of Mr Raouf Abujabber, owner of Tell el-Umeiri West, we were able to examine also materials from a recent study of the Abujabber homestead, Yadoudeh, and its environs (Franken, 1979), which lie within the MPP Survey Area. The MPP Survey aims at intensive coverage of the five-kilometer radius from Umeiri, with extensive coverage out to a ten-kilometer radius. The intensive survey (Map 4) thus overlaps the northeast segment of the Hesban Survey, where the latter had included 29 sites (nos. 126-155 in Ibach 1981); few of these were revisited in 1984. 'Site-seeking' could instead be focused, first season, in the northern quadrants, which are most seriously threatened now by urban sprawl. As additional control, we plotted the entire area for intensive survey into squares of 200 × 200 m. (nearly 2000 total) and used the table of random numbers. Examination of 38 'Random Squares' took the team to just about every conceivable variation in geographical and social location: from densely urban (Naur; Kh. es-Suq) to villages (el-Buneiyyat North, el-Buneiyyat South, Umm el-Basatin), to large family villas (Yadoudeh, Bilas), to tent encampments; and from densely wooded hills to broad fields (some tilled, some fallow). None of the Random Squares was devoid of artifactual evidence, mostly, of course, potsherds.

Results of the pottery readings from the random sample (Figure 6) turned out to be closely comparable to the Hesban Survey results, summarized above in Figure 5.

38 Random Squares	
Middle Bronze II	2 squares (5.3%)
Late Bronze	-----
Iron I	9 squares (23.7%)

Figure 6. Madaba Plains Survey: Random Sample

In addition to the random sampling, the MPP Survey recorded data on 55 'sites', newly examined in 1984. Results appear, at first glance, to be less comparable:

55 sites	
Middle Bronze II	2 sites (3.6%)
Late Bronze	3 'possible' (5.5%)
Iron I	12 sites (21.8%)

Figure 7. Madaba Plains Survey: Sites

The contrast disappears when we count, in MB II, three of the Hesban Survey sites which fall within the five-kilometer radius from Umeiri, including Umeiri West. Similarly, while the three 'LB' readings noted above are only 'possible' (one sherd in each case!), three of the LB sites in Hesban Survey, including Umeiri West, lie within the overlapping area.

The survey evidence for Umeiri's domination of the entire area in MB-LB tends to undergird its equation with toponym #95-96 (*Krmn*) in the list of Thutmose III and the proposed identification with biblical Abel-Keramim in Judg. 11.33 (Redford 1982). But the identification must remain tentative. There is an early Islamic 'Abila' in the wider neighborhood, for which Umeiri lies too far west (Knauf 1984).

At least thirty-two of the fifty-five 'sites' examined in 1984 appear to be farmsteads, reflecting two periods of most intensive agricultural exploration of the region: first, throughout the Iron age, and again in the Roman-Byzantine era (Geraty et al.).

When taken together with the results of excavations described above, the returns from these two intensive surveys of overlapping regions south of Amman correlate very well with the earlier extensive survey in northern Jordan and the Jordan Valley Survey. From the Yarmuq in the north to the Mujib in the south it is not the number of settlements that changes significantly in the transition from the Middle Bronze to the Late Bronze period. What changes drastically, with a few exceptions of older fortified towns, is their locations, strong evidence for shifting makeup and alignments of small population groups, throughout most of the Late Bronze Age.

Especially hard times, mostly politically induced, at the end of the Middle Bronze period and continuing throughout the Late Bronze Age, precipitated emigration, out of Cisjordan and the broad flanks of the Jordan River and its northern tributaries, to the Jordanian plateau. There, except for the region south of the 'Grand Canyon' (Wadi Mujib), the settled population is found newly grouped at widely separated towns. Where the towns are walled we may suspect that an older city-state polity has persisted from the Middle Bronze period or has recently been transplanted to a new setting. It is clear, from the biblical onomasticon that many newcomers to Transjordan in the Late Bronze period had arrived from the far north. These latter were also known originally as 'westerners' (Amorites) from Mesopotamian perspective.

Chapter 2

THE BIBLICAL TRADITION IN CONTEXT

Transjordan in recent history-writing

Egyptian records, including the Amarna correspondence, provide a picture for only parts of our area; and even those parts are not always in focus. The few 'Late Bronze' place names mentioned for Transjordan, at Amarna and in the pharaohs' itineraries after Thutmose III, are all found in the far north. The southernmost city is Pella. Prior to Ramesses II, there are no settlements mentioned south of a line between Pella in the west and Bozra in the east. Even with Ramesses II, only one reference occurs, and that is to 'the *Shasu*-country of Seir' (Edom).

This strong evidence for Egyptian interests concentrated in northern Transjordan, combined with the alleged gap in sedentary occupation from the Jabboq to the Arnon in the Middle Bronze II and Late Bronze I periods, is significant to both sides of the debate over Israelite origins which has continued throughout most of this century, especially intense in the wake of M. Noth's historical reconstruction (Noth 1960). Unable to accept a blanket equation of biblical 'Hebrews' with the Habiru/Apiru mentioned frequently in extrabiblical sources from the Middle and Late Bronze periods, Noth held that the twelve-part organization of old Israel resembled an amphictyonic league, constituted primarily out of religious loyalty to a central sanctuary. Such leagues are better known in later classical sources from the Aegean world. The analogous 'all Israel' tradition only crystallized on the soil of Canaan, according to Noth, out of a prolonged process which saw the sedentarization of nomadic clans and tribes, over perhaps several centuries, each group contributing singly, or in small constituent alliances, its own tradition. On this view, there simply was no 'Israel' to have a history until, early to mid-thirteenth century BCE, unless it was a considerably smaller league of, say, six tribes (Newman 1962; Smend 1970).

Noth's work began an epoch in the study of biblical historiography which has not ended. There is much, in fact, to be said for Noth's general reconstruction of early Israelite history in the Transjordan. That, according to Noth, had involved slow but, cumulatively, large-scale migration from west to east. Some excerpts:

> ... the 'house of Joseph' was a particularly large association of clans holding the whole of the central part of the mountains west of the Jordan... The great association of the 'house of Joseph' (obviously originally a personal name) was in fact divided in Palestine itself into two tribes, Manasseh and Ephraim, of which *Ephraim* was the greater and more important (Noth 1960: 59). The name 'Ephraim' is obviously not a personal name, but the name of a place.... (Noth 1960: 60). Quite early on, the vigorous tribe of Ephraim was no longer satisfied... west of the Jordan... And so Ephraimite families went over the Jordan Valley into the central part of the country east of Jordan (Noth 1960: 61). The other tribe which established itself within the framework of the 'house of Joseph' as Ephraim's northern neighbor, seems to have had a rather complicated history. The Song of Deborah, one of the oldest passages in the Old Testament, mentions (Judges v. 14) *Machir* as well as Ephraim... But the tribe of Machir—or at any rate the main part of it—then migrated to the land east of Jordan...; the people who remained in the land west of the Jordan on the northern borders of Ephraim formed the tribe of *Manasseh*, which is clearly a personal name... thus Machir became the 'father of Gilead'... The greater importance of the west Jordan possessions ... was marked by the fact that 'Manasseh' now became the real tribal name and—without regard to the actual historical process—Machir was subordinated to Manasseh genealogically and made its son... (Noth 1960: 61-62)... The tribe of Gad, which lived in the land east of the Jordan..., alone among the tribes of Israel, probably made a permanent settlement there from the beginning, ... (Noth 1958: 63).... Reuben is always mentioned in connection with Gad...; but the details indicate that those references are not based on any clear-cut conception of a particular territory belonging to the tribe of Reuben but rather that the land of Gad was always theoretically divided in various ways, half of it being allotted to Reuben... Originally the tribe of Reuben resided, not in the land east of the Jordan, but somewhere or other west of the Jordan (Noth 1960: 63-64).

There is little or nothing in these excerpts from Noth's reconstruction which critical scholars today reject as implausible. The most serious inadequacy has turned out to be the notion of the amphictyony and the a priori rejection of any prior unity of constituencies called 'Israel', or bearing the same 'tribal' names, except in much smaller, local combinations. The historical reconstruction is thus lacking in any suggestion of motivation for the emergence of the wide-ranging twelve-tribe organization, making such sweeping territorial claims in the twelfth to eleventh centuries BCE.

That a rigorous application of the methods of 'Traditions-History' lacked adequate controls for confidently assessing Israel's protohistory was the burden of John Bright's monograph, *Early Israel in Recent History Writing* (1956). Were the stories of the ancestors (Genesis 12–50) entirely pious anachronism? Bright was far more impressed by parallels in law, social custom, and onomastics, between the world of the patriarchs (our Earliest Israel) and the extra-biblical sources from the eighteenth to fifteenth centuries BCE, especially at Mari and Nuzi. Bright also argued for a high correlation between biblical conquest stories and archaeological destruction layers from the thirteenth and twelfth centuries in Cisjordan. He also continued over the years to assert a Hebrew/Habiru connection, but not in the sense of the blanket 'ethnic' equation rejected by many others (Bright 1981: 45-103).

Bright's widely influential synthesis has in turn been called into question by the partial liquidation (through clarification and reinterpretation) of parallels, especially from Nuzi (Thompson 1974; Van Seters 1975) and the broad time span represented by the pertinent 'destructions'. The latter could scarcely be compressed into one commander's lifetime. Are the destruction layers evidence for the historicity of biblical 'conquest' claims? Or do they rather represent (especially the earlier ones) a situation to which Early Israel was the response and outcome? In my work on Joshua and Judges (Boling 1975; 1982), I became increasingly convinced that there is a high admixture of both realities behind the stories.

G.E. Mendenhall's argument for a similar alternative is quite compatible with Noth's reconstruction, as far as the latter goes.

> The biblical traditions give no hint of migrations during this period from any other source than Egypt, and the only demonstrable source of accessions is from the population who were already

> settled on the land.... Since the entire area had very little if any sedentary occupation before about 1300 BC, the events may be reconstructed as follows. With the increasing social and political instability in Palestine proper..., groups migrated to the fringe areas from the more populous regions to the West and North. The close connections of the Reubenites with Palestine proper have been noted by Martin Noth. Immediately the Moabite and Edomite kingdoms erected border fortresses, found by Nelson Glueck, to preserve their territorial integrity; these people cannot have been far removed culturally and linguistically from the group called Reuben. Migrations from the North brought organized military gangs (like that of Jephthah later), who established a military domination over the area which was populated by similar migrations from the central and northern parts of Palestine as well as migrations from the north and northeast. The military kingdoms of Sihon and Og were destroyed... but those of Moab and Edom were not even attacked... Sihon did attack, for in the meantime the population of his kingdom had been attracted by and perhaps already had joined the religious community of Israel; his army would consist of the professional soldiers who owed personal allegiance to him... Therefore the defeat was possible because of the support of a large part of the villagers and shepherds of the region (Mendenhall 1962: 81-82).

In Chapter 1, we have dealt at length with the alleged gap in sedentary occupation prior to the thirteenth century and, more briefly, with the problematical 'Edomite border fortresses'. Apart from these, Mendenhall's proposal wears well. In 1962 the pace of archaeological work in Transjordan was still far outdistanced by the work in western Palestine, where, especially since 1948, archaeology has emerged as something like the national hobby. But the pace of archaeology on the East Bank, especially survey work, is rapidly closing large gaps. At the same time, attention to vicissitudes of 'tradition' continues to underline the problematic character of many biblical texts as reliable carriers of historical memory. This will be very clear to anyone who has read all the way through N. Gottwald's massive work, *The Tribes of Yahweh* (1979).

Gottwald, I think, puts the last nail in the coffin of the religious-amphictyony-without-much-secular-jurisdiction, à la Noth. Yet, surprisingly, Gottwald retains the old analytical base: originally separated and largely unrelated sacral traditions contributed by various distinct population groups.

We turn next, therefore, to a closer review of pertinent biblical texts in recent scholarship, and problems of historical geography.

Kingdoms of Sihon and Og: Num. 20.14–21.35; Deut. 2.1–3.11; Judg. 11.12-28

The complex issues of traditionary development and problems of literary dependence are probably nowhere more formidable than in the 'memory' of Sihon and Og. For the most part, Sihon and Og appear to be presented in the tradition as contemporaries, controlling, in the simplest form of the tradition, the territory 'from the valley of Arnon unto Mount Sirion (that is, Hermon)' (Deut. 4.46; cf. 31.4; Josh. 2.10; 9.10). 'But we may suspect that this Deuteronomic tradition of the two kings as contemporary Amorite kings is the end product of a long tradition whose history and origins need examination' (Bartlett 1970: 258). As Bartlett sees it, the story begins in very old sources which may be only vaguely discerned in the extant account.

More recently it has been suggested that since the kingdom of Amurru (=Amorite) appears as a political designation 'only in the Amarna and subsequent Hittite sources', the kingdom of Sihon the Amorite in Transjordan was very likely a transplanted survival of a regime, possibly represented at Amarna by Abdi-Ashirta, after destruction of Ugarit by the Sea Peoples (Mendenhall 1973: 160). It is a suggestion which at least fits the archaeological picture, as drawn above, for the Transjordan highlands in the first half of the Late Bronze Age. Except for the 'Moab' plateau, where the number of settlements was rapidly growing, the picture from the Arnon to the Yarmuq throughout Late Bronze is that of a sedentary population at about the same level as in MB II, but in mostly new and different locations. If Sihon is the best remembered, it may mean simply that he was the most 'successful' in mobilizing opposition to Early Israel. Obviously only 'maybe', in the current state of our knowledge.

For the location of Sihon's kingdom Bartlett had at least one fixed point in the ancient song of Num. 21.27-30 which designates Heshbon as 'the city of Sihon' (*qiryat-sihon*). The location was long thought to be marked by Tell Hesban, but that is now out of the question, as indicated above in Chapter 1. According to the preceding prose, Sihon had ruled 'from the Arnon to the Jabboq' bordered by the Ammonites on the east (Num. 21.24). If Jahaz, where Sihon attacked Israel, is to be sought either in the region between Madaba and Dibon (Noth 1968: 163) or at el-Medeineyeh al-Thamad (see now, Dearman 1984), 'then perhaps Sihon's kingdom reached not to the Arnon but only to the *wadi eth-thamad* and its lower reaches, the *wadi el-wala* and *wadi el-heidan*' (Bartlett 1970: 259-60).

Noth long ago suggested that the phrase 'from the Arnon to the Jabboq' first appears in secondary additions to Deuteronomic tradition, from the sixth-century Persian administration of the territory as part of the province of Ammon (Noth 1941: 50ff., 53f.). Bartlett was inclined to agree that the phrase is 'part of a Deuteronomic simplification which divided the land east of the Jordan into two kingdoms, one ruled by Sihon and one by Og...' (Bartlett 1970: 260). 'From Arnon to the Jabboq' may well be a rhetorical summary which minimizes the concentration of Ammonites near the source of the Jabboq, for which Bartlett has archaeological evidence in the Marqa Airport 'Temple' (firm) and the alleged Ammonite border 'towers' (problematical). In any case, both the northern and southern extent of Sihon's territory remain unclarified.

The Kingdom of Og in Bashan is even more elusive. Its fullest description is in Joshua 12. Og reigned at Ashtaroth and Edrei: 'ruling the land from Mount Hermon (actually from Salecah) over the whole of Bashan to the border of the Geshurites and the Maacathites (that is, half of Gilead), as far as the border of Sihon, king of Heshbon' (Josh. 12.4b-5, Tr. AB 6). The text, twice glossed, probably belongs to the later stratum of the Dtr corpus (Boling 1982: 248-49). Here it is the southern border that fails to inspire confidence. In strictly geographical terms:

> Bounded on the west by the edge of the plateau, Bashan extends in the north to the foot of Hermon, in the south across the Yarmuq to the mountains of Gilead some six miles beyond the present Irbid-Mafraq road, and on the east to the black, volcanic mass of Jebel Druze (Baly 1957: 220).

Among the chief towns of Bashan, Ashtaroth (Deut. 1.4; Josh. 9.10; 12.4; 13.12, 31; 1 Chr. 6.71) is identified with Tell Ashtarah. Edrei (Deut. 1.4; 3.10; Num. 21.33; Josh. 12.4; 13.12, 31) must be at or near Der'a in the valley of the upper Yarmuq. Salecah (Deut. 3.10; Josh. 12.5; 13.11; 1 Chr. 5.11) is perhaps modern Salkhad. The name of Golan (Deut. 4.43; Josh. 20.8; 1 Chr. 6.71) seems to be represented in Sahem el-Jolan, about fifteen kilometers northwest of Der'a.

Here we have at least a roster of place names, some of which also occur with surprising frequency in extra-biblical sources. A 'ruler of

Ashtaroth' is mentioned on a figurine from the Egyptian Middle Kingdom, c. nineteenth century (ANET[2]: 329, n. 8). Thutmose III in the fifteenth century lists Ashtaroth and Edrei among his conquests (ANET[2]: 242). One Ayyub prince of Ashtaroth, is mentioned by the prince of Pella, asserting to Pharaoh the loyalty of both princes, in a fourteenth-century Amarna Letter (ANET[2]: 486, Letter #246). It appears that on another occasion (Amarna Letter #197) Ashtaroth sent chariotry to the side of the Hittites (Bartlett 1970; 267, n. 4).

Despite the evidence for a record of LB intrigue centering especially in Ashtaroth and Edrei, it has been widely held, following Noth, that in the biblical material the story of Og is deuteronomistic from the beginning, appearing first in Deut. 3.1-11 (Bartlett 1970: 266), which has a reflex in Num. 21.33-35, 'no doubt itself a later supplementary addition' (von Rad 1966: 44).

While it might not be unreasonable to think that 'The Israelites encountered king Og of Bashan in stories emanating from the city-state territory of Bashan but not directly as historical figure' (Noth 1960: 159-60), Bartlett found it hard to deny all historicity to the Edrei battle reference (Num. 21.33; Deut. 3.1). Furthermore, the non-Semitic name of Og is now compared with Hittite and Luwian Ḫuḫḫa, and later Lycian *Kuga* (Mendenhall 1973: 160).

Another notice about Og, found only in the latest stratum of the Dtr-corpus (Deut. 3.11), identifies Og as the last of the 'Rephaim'. The word is best explained as referring, originally, to an aristocracy of military professionals; from whose ranks also came many of the Canaanite kings (see Boling 1982: 325 and references). That Og was the last of the Rephaim, in the original sense, may well be historically correct. The development of a legendary sense, 'giants', was doubtless spurred on by such 'evidence', as Og's massive (costly) iron bedframe, for a long time on public display at the Ammonite capital (Deut. 3.11). 'It seems a fair guess that the solution... lies in postulating that Og was known differently to two different groups of Israelites' (Barlett 1970: 268). The brief description in Deut. 3.11, together with all the other antiquarian notes in Deuteronomy 1-3, suggests a southern or Judahite provenance. Bartlett concluded that a vague southern memory of Og 'has been combined... in the final introduction to the book of Deuteronomy with more detailed traditions coming from sources to whom Og was a less shadowy figure' (1970: 270-71).

Whatever the original (or maximal) extent of the 'Kingdom of Og in Bashan', its southern limit has been obscured by subsequent developments in 'Gilead'. The land of Gilead in biblical texts falls between and often overlaps in part the territories of Sihon and Og. To what did 'Gilead' originally refer?

Khirbet Jel'ad in the hills south of the Jabboq may preserve in part the name Mizpeh-Gilead of Judg. 11.29; cf. Mizpah in Gen. 31.48; Judg. 10.17 (de Vaux 1941: 27ff.). Others opt for Reshuni, several kilometers northwest of Khirbet Jel'ad for the biblical site (Noth 1960: 158). But 'Gilead' most often refers to a *region*, north of the Jabboq. It may be a correct supposition that early 'Israelite' immigrants from the west first extended the reference northwards, with such town names as Jabesh-Gilead, Ramoth-Gilead, and Tishbeh-Gilead (Noth 1960: 61-62). On the other hand,

> It is possible that we are too quick to see the river Jabboq as dividing areas (as does the Deuteronomist in his schematization) when we should see the river as the central feature of the one mountain range of Gilead, lying between Irbid in the north and Heshbon in the south, between Og in Bashan and Sihon on the plain (Bartlett 1970: 263).

If it thus appears likely that the traditions about Sihon and Og were originally separate and perhaps unrelated, how was it (or where was it) that they were combined in a pre-Deuteronomistic 'authority'? Was it in liturgical material stemming from influential sanctuaries perhaps frequented by both 'Gileadites' and 'Gadites' (e.g. Mizpeh of Gilead, or Gilgal near Jericho)? The Gilgal sanctuary has been nominated as a very likely candidate, in the wake of studies by A. Alt, M. Noth, G. von Rad, H.-J. Kraus, and K. Galling (Bartlett 1970: 273, n. 1), to which we should now add F.M. Cross (1973: 79-142). Nor can one rule out places such as the Late Bronze period sanctuary at Tell Deir 'Alla, near the mouth of the Jabboq (Franken 1969). A tradition of Balaam the Seer, another newcomer from the far north, was very much alive at Deir 'Alla, long after the place revived, deep into the Iron II period (see now McCarter 1980).

I have described at some length, and commented on, Bartlett's attempt to unravel the history of the Sihon and Og traditions because it is an impressive and often persuasive effort, which has called forth detailed response and continuing debate. J. Van Seters (1972) holds out for further literary analysis. Finding to his satisfaction that Num. 21.21-35 is the work of a redactor who used Deuteronomy as one of the sources for constructing these episodes, Van Seters is sure that the search for antecedents must end there, with one exception not canvassed by Bartlett.

> ... virtually the whole of the Num. 21.21-25 text is to be found in Deut 2.26-27, though the Numbers version is much shorter. The same is true for the account of the battle with Og ... in which Num 21.35 is a considerable abbreviation of Deut 3.3-10. Only the messenger speech of Num 21.22 departs significantly from that of Deut 2.27-29, as well as the references to Israel's settlement in Num 21.25 which is not found in Deuteronomy. However, for the rest the two versions are so close in basic content and wording that one must depend on the other or both derive from a common literary tradition (Van Seters 1972: 184).

The question, then, becomes how to account for the quite remarkable differences. In addition to the different messenger speech, in Numbers neither Moses nor God nor any divine intervention is mentioned; and Numbers goes beyond the defeat of Sihon to Israel's settlement in the region (v. 25).

The proposed solution is to find in Numbers also the influence of Jephthah's negotiations with the Ammonites (Judg. 11.19-26), concluding that the Sihon version of Numbers is a conflation of sources, '... two deuteronomistic versions which are extant in the texts of Deut 2.26-37 and Judg 11.19-26' (Van Seters 1972: 189). The problem of the different messenger speech in Num. 21.22 shows that influence of the Judges account also appears in the request for passage through Edom (Num. 20.14-21). There 'the narrator-redactor attempted to modify' the account of Deuteronomy, which implied permission granted, to show complete refusal 'in conformity with another version, that of Judg. 11.12-22' (Van Seters 1972: 191).

The keystone in Van Seters's arch of literary reconstruction is a comparison of the poetic fragment celebrating Sihon's victories in Num. 21.27-30 and the remarkably similar taunt song, aimed at Moab, in Jer. 48.45-46. If 'there is no good reason to isolate this taunt song from similar ones contained in this prophetic literature of the late monarchy and early exilic periods', it must indicate a very late contribution to the account in Numbers (Van Seters 1972: 194). As Van Seters reads it, the identity of the Sihon mentioned in the nuclear poem is, by itself, unclear. It was only a later redactor of Numbers who made explicit identification in an extra-metrical addition to Num. 21.29, 'to the King of the Amorites, Sihon', which is missing in the Jeremiah parallel.

Each of the three Sihon accounts is seen by Van Seters to function in a different way in its own context. In Deuteronomy the account gives theological legitimacy to ancient boundaries and territorial claims. In the 'later' Jephthah story there is a sharp polemical shift, versus Ammon in particular. The 'latest' version, Numbers, no longer betrays the deuteronomistic theological tendency. 'If anything, it secularizes the account', perhaps sharing in the implications of Ezek. 47.13-23 that the eastern region no longer belongs to the Israel of restoration vision. If so, 'On the historical level the conquest of the kingdoms of Sihon and Og must be regarded with grave suspicion' (Van Seters 1972: 196-97), thus compounding several times over any quest for Early Israel in Transjordan. I share the objection that Van Seters's approach begs a question, in favor of literary versus oral forms (Gunn 1974).

The debate has continued through another two rounds (Van Seters 1976 versus Gunn 1976; Bartlett 1978 versus Van Seters 1980), and surely demonstrates that so long as the discussion is limited to questions of literary dependence, it might have gone either way. For in either case, whether priority is assigned to Deuteronomy or to old narrative sources behind Numbers, the result is a redactor leaving in the finished work what a recent seminarian labels 'bonehead infelicities'. It is equally possible, if not more probable, that the redactors were not all that familiar with *all* of the literary texts of their predecessors.

In his final response to Bartlett, Van Seters returns to the Jeremiah setting of the taunt song shared with Numbers 21. Here I would suggest that the context does not augur well for the poem's late origin. As the climactic unit in the long section of poetic woe oracles versus Moab (Jer. 48.1-47), interspersed with presumably later prose oracles, one gets the impression that this one has been around for a long time. The isolated line in Jer. 48.45a, 'In the shadow of Heshbon the fugitives/Halt, all spent' (tr. Bright 1965: 319) is not poetry (contra Van Seters 1972: 194). It may be read, rather, as the compiler's setting of a scene in which a traditional taunt is still recited, and in which setting the phrase 'to the King of Amorites, Sihon' is obviously no longer appropriate. But, according to the final verse, it will not always be so, for 'yet I will restore the fortunes of Moab . . . ' (Jer. 48.47); and the well-established practice of taunting, on the basis of tradition, will end! The collection of traditional taunts against Ammonites (Jer. 49.1-6) concludes similarly. But, significantly, the traditional taunts against Edom (Jer. 49.7-32) do not have such a happy ending, perhaps due to continuing hostilities, to be represented finally by Edom's pillaging of post-587 Jerusalem and Judah

(Obadiah), which contemporary Moab and Ammon were probably in no condition to emulate (see Obadiah; Ps. 137.7; Ezek. 35).

In his second article Van Seters was able also to appeal to the archaeological work in Tell Hesban, after five field seasons of work there, beginning in 1968.

> It has now become clear that there could have been no ancient Amorite kingdom at Heshbon either in the Late Bronze Age or the early Iron Age and that only in the rather late monarchical period did a city arise that was large enough to be considered as a royal city (Van Seters 1980: 118).

But the argument assumes an identification which is now open to question. The excavators at Tell Hesban may rather have dug up another example of how place names move around, sometimes under the press of environmental change and historical circumstances (cf. the Arad-Hormah problems in the Negeb), sometimes for convenience of religious pilgrimage (e.g. the frequent difficulty of harmonizing Eusebius's Onomasticon (reflecting the situation of the early Common Era) with location of pre-Roman ruins and historical sources. A good candidate for the earlier Heshbon might be the imposing mound of Tell Jalul (Map 3, site 26), with clear LB and Iron I surface pottery (Ibach 1978b), five kilometers east of Madaba and the 'King's Highway', the latter running much closer to Tell Hesban.

Yet another substantial treatment of our subject, and one which addresses more directly the range of archaeological data, is M. Weippert's contribution to the *Symposia Celebrating the Seventy-fifth Anniversary of ASOR*, 'The Israelite "Conquest" and the evidence from Transjordan' (Weippert 1979). Here, however, the discussion or prose narrative texts, and problems of their interrelationship, is very brief. Weippert assumes the priority of the story line in Numbers and does not address the matter of Deuteronomic influence, noting only that 'Deuteronomy 2 presents an interesting variation'. Jephthah's lesson in history given to the king of the Ammonites, however, 'is obviously dependent on Numbers 21-23' (Weippert 1979: 16).

After noting that the book of Numbers contains a few accounts of conflicts with Moabites (in apparent contradiction to one branch of the story line), namely the Balaam unit (Num. 22.2–24.25) and the incident at the shrine of Baal-Peor (Num. 25), Weippert turns his attention to the much older poems from 'The Book of the Wars of

Yahweh' (Num. 21.14-15) and the *mashal*-singers (Num. 21.27-31). These Weippert considers unquestionably old and probably pre-monarchical (Weippert 1979: 17).

The first of these two song fragments was at last clarified, Weippert agrees, by D.L. Christensen (1974: 360), whose translation reads:

> Yahweh came in a whirlwind;
> He came to the branch wadis of the Arnon.
> He marched through the wadis;
> He {marched / turned aside} to the seat of Ar.
> He leaned toward the border of Moab
> ....

According to this reading, Yahweh's advance was *into border territory* (better to render 'toward', I suggest, in both lines 4 and 5, strictly parallel construction), where tributary wadis of the Arnon would pose a problem of ill-defined borders, in contrast to the deep rift of the Mujib after their confluence.

Weippert's suggested improvement in the last three lines makes a violation of Moabite territory indisuputable, but the result is far less satisfactory as early poetry:

> Crossed the river, crossed it
> Deviated (from the way) to dwell in Ar,
> established himself in the land of Moab.
> (Weippert 1979: 17).

But where was Ar? And was Ar the Moabite capital at the time? Neither Christensen nor Weippert is concerned with these questions. Ar is most often located by geographers at el-Misna', some 14 miles south of the Mujib. But both this text and Deut. 2.18 suggest a location much nearer the Arnon. Parallelism in the song is at this point such as to prompt even a suggestion that Ar was not a town but a region (Simons 1959: 435). One thing is clear, however. The poetic fragment was taken up by the narrator in Numbers 21 *because* it put the Moabite border at the Arnon.

> The picture here is that of the Divine Warrior poised on the edge of the promised land ... He has come ... with his hosts to the sources of the River Arnon in Transjordan. He marches through the wadis, turning aside to settle affairs with Moab before marching against the Amorite kings to the north ... (Christensen 1974: 360).

In this song fragment, if the last two lines are closely parallel ('toward'), there is no assertion of invading Moabite *territory*. Rather, Moab is allowed to see that Israel on the move through Transjordan would be well protected.

Weippert's treatment of the Sihon fragment (Num. 21.27-30) is more substantial. He must, however, resort to radical surgery before concluding that the original referent of 'Sihon' in v. 28 is totally obscure and was only made to refer to 'Sihon the Amorite' in the prose narrative. Van Seters was on the right track but had not gone far enough! The prose emerges from Weippert's analysis too as very questionable historical tradition. Rather, 'It is highly probable that this account is based on a fabrication or, to put it less harshly, that it was deduced from the designation of Heshbon as *qryt-syhn*' in the poem (Weippert 1979: 22).

Weippert does not claim to understand v. 30 and wisely leaves it untranslated, observing only that it appears to recall a defeat of 'Moab' in which the towns of Dibon and Madaba were removed from Moabite control. See his discussion of formidable textual problems (Weippert 1979: 18 and 20, n. 19). It is important to note, however, that Dibon and Madaba both lie well to the north of the Arnon.

I do not agree that v. 27b should be subtracted, to find the original poem:

> Come to Heshbon, let it be built;
> Let Sihon-town be established.

This is cast in strict horizontal and grammatical parallelism, like the bulk of vv. 28-29a and unlike the prose substitutions which appropriately introduce another rendition of the song in Jer. 48.45a. Here the initial reference to *'ir sihon* also stands in vertical parallelism with *qiryat-sihon*, 'village' (perhaps better 'castle') 'of Sihon', in v. 28a. This is a characteristically old poetic A-word/B-word pattern, with the shorter A-word often more common in prose (Boling 1960).

Nor is it clear that Weippert and others are correct in regarding the last segment of v. 29, 'to the King of the Amorites, Sihon', as secondary. If the rest of vv. 29b-30 are in fact poetry, then it is at least as possible that something has dropped out, triggering much of the textual confusion.

In Weippert's view it is the reference to Ar in v. 28 that connects this song fragment with the one in vv. 14b-15 and indicates a violation of Moabite territory: by Early Israel in the original (if

Weippert is correct) but by Sihon the Amorite in the ancient redactor's 'deduction'. However, it is precisely here that MT in vv. 27b-29a presents the most serious departure from otherwise tight poetic structure, with the shift from singular (*ʿr*) to plural (*bʿly*) and from one lexical category (place name) to another (social status). In early spelling the plural construct form of *ʿr* 'towns' would be indistinguishable from the place name *ʿr* 'Ar'. We may therefore confidently recognize the latter vocalization in v. 17a as contamination from the preceding and proper vocalization in v. 15 (Noth 1968: 161 Hanson 1968: 300-301).

The entire poem thus comes into sharper focus. It is all about towns *north of the recognized Moab border at the Arnon*, towns which had changed hands at least twice in the era just preceding or during the advent of Early Israel. An initial Moabite expansion to the north (providing a setting for Early Israel's conflicts with Moabites in the Balaam and Baal-Peor materials of Numbers 22–25) was partially cancelled out by Sihon's conquests from a headquarters at Heshbon, which is now to be sought somewhere in the wider reaches of the Madaba Plains. The poem does not begin with a celebration of Heshbon's destruction. Instead, it anticipates Heshbon's expansion:

27b Come to Heshbon, let it be built up;
Let Sihon-town be established.
28 For fire went forth from Heshbon,
Flame from Sihon-village.
It consumed towns of Moab,
Lords of Arnon Heights.
29 Woe to you, O Moab!
You are ruined, people of Chemosh!
He has made his sons fugitives,
And his daughters captives.
30 ....
....

The only reference to Sihon's (or simply the Amorites'?) original seizure of Heshbon is, perhaps, in the badly garbled v. 30.

There remains the question of what interest the *mashal*-singers of Early Israel would have in an old Amorite victory song. 'The biblical writers would normally have had no interest whatsoever in such a victory, let alone the songs of victory of enemies long since conquered' (Weippert 1979: 21). I suppose it depends on what counts as 'normal'. The context is one of conflicting territorial claims, making such a song a very 'normal' interest if you live in the disputed neighborhood. 'The most likely explanation of the inclusion of the poem in the Israelite tradition is the assumption that the event involved the interests of the group who preserved it' (Mendenhall 1962: 81), in this case, we may suppose, the local populace who had subsequently rid themselves of Sihon's domination by a transfer of allegiance to Yahweh and the organization of Early Israel.

Everything seems to turn upon what counted for membership in Early Israel, a question which is simply finessed in all approaches which begin with the peoples unity via some process of 'religious ethnogenesis', following upon a population explosion in the hills of Western Palestine at the Late Bronze—Early Iron Age Transition (Weippert 1979: 33). Such is the thesis developed by Weippert in his excellent earlier monograph on the settlement of the Israelite tribes (Weippert 1971) and reiterated in the essay under review here.

The conclusion that Num. 21.28-29 is a misunderstood or misused victory song reinforced for Weippert the work of his predecessors (Noth 1968: 164-65, and especially Mittmann 1973: 143-49), who likewise concluded that Num. 21.14-21 is a late redactional compilation without any basis in early tradition. Together with the Sihon story and poem, these verses are seen to bridge a 'geographical gap between the wilderness tradition and the Benjaminite conquest tradition', the latter with the starting point in the *'rbwt mw'b* 'Plains of Moab' (Weippert 1979: 23).

But if the putative 'gap' in traditions corresponds in general to a gap in Egyptian references to most of Transjordan, and if it also corresponds to a period of severe demographic reshuffling as shown above in Chapter 1, then it is likely that the more serious 'gap' resides in a history-of-traditions methodology too rigidly applied. In this case the problem is the assumption of an 'ethnic' homogeneity in Israelite origins ('pastoral nomadism', which actually designates *social location*), which is undercut by the survival of contrasting memories from very turbulent times (see below, on 'ethnogenesis').

Thus far I have agreed with Weippert and others that the Late Bronze-Iron I picture in Transjordan picture described by Glueck now needs considerable modification in detail. More and more Late Bronze Age sites are being reported South of the Pella-Bozrah line. The reason for Egyptian silence regarding much of the area south of Pella is thus not an absence of settlements, but the absence of Egyptian provincial administrators (Weippert 1979: 26). It was in this area of administrative vacuum that the first of the Iron Age territorial states was consolidated in the narrow Canaan-Transjordan corridor between the desert and the sea. The first territorial state, Moab, was effectively isolated and protected by the two 'Grand Canyons', Wadi Mujib and Wadi Hasa. A setting in the 13th century (probably well along in that century) is now strongly supported by Miller's survey of the 'Moabite' plateau.

Excursus on Moab, Land and 'Legitimacy'

Having once written that 'Moab' could be used as 'a geographical designation for all inhabitable land east of the Dead Sea and west of the desert' (Boling 1975a: 205), I now see that I was probably mistaken. The statement was much too broad. 'Plains of Moab' (*'rbwt mw'b*) in biblical usage encompasses only the western brink of the plateau, where the escarpment is broken by deep wadis descending into the Arabah at the northeastern shore of the Dead Sea. This geographical term occurs nine times in Numbers 22–36 (22.1; 26.3, 63; 31.12; 33.48, 49, 50; 35.1; 36.13), twice in Deuteronomy's narrative conclusion (Deut. 34.1, 8) and once in Josh. 13.32; but nowhere else in the Hebrew Bible.

There is no text in scripture referring to the premonarchy period that confers political legitimacy on the application of 'Moab(ite)' to any *territory* north of the Arnon, with the possible exception of Jephthah's message to the king of the Ammonites in Judg. 11.24. Scripture referring to the same period does indeed remember *Moabite occupation* north of the Arnon but considers it illegitimate.

The situation in Judges 11 is notoriously difficult. Says Jephthah to the king of the Ammonites:

> Is it not right that whatever your god Chemosh expropriates for you, you should possess; and that everything Yahweh our God expropriates for us, we should possess? (Judg. 11.24 tr. Boling 1975).

Inasmuch as the chief god of Moab, Chemosh, is here invoked (and not the Ammonite deity Milcom), literary critics have generally concluded that an account originally involving Israel and Moab has been turned imperfectly into an account of Israel versus the Ammonites. While such is not inconceivable, the extant version is entirely free of the reflective glossing that such transformation of tradition frequently evoked. The implication of Jephthah's speech is that Ammonites at the desert fringe had also reacted successfully to a northward expansion of Moab. Was it in collaboration with their western, Amorite, neighbors? Is that why Og's bedstead was said to be at Rabbah?

If the Ammonites were treating the erstwhile 'Moabite' territory as a separate entity, administratively and diplomatically, the jurisdiction of the god Chemosh might well be generally recognized for diplomatic purposes. They may even have maintained that the disputed territory was held in trust for Moabite claimants (Boling 1975: 201-204). In any case, the disputed territory cannot have been very extensive, after Early Israel's consolidation in the territory of Sihon's former kingdom, and was considered from Jepthah's side to be not worth fighting over, except in Israel's self defense. So far as we can tell, Jephthah's victory did not lead to any expanded territorial claims, at Ammonite expense.

The situation changed drastically toward the end of the eleventh century, with the monarchical transformation of Israelite religion and polity. The territory of the Transjordan kingdoms became, thereafter, fair game.

Early Israel: Yahwist Newcomers and Village-Farmer Sympathizers

Outside the Bible, Moab is mentioned for the first time, in extant sources, early in the reign of Ramesses II. The name occurs with the representation of a fortress, on the east wall in the court of Ramesses at the Luxor Temple. According to the inscription it is 'The town which the mighty arm of Pharaoh plundered in the land of Moab, *btrt*'. Where was *btrt*? Both Khirbet el-Medeiniyeh (near Lejjun) and el-Misna' (near Rabbah) are plausible suggestions (Kitchen 1964: 52, 62-65). Since the representation at Luxor is stereotypical, it is not clear whether *btrt* in Moab was large or small, fortified or open settlement.

The earliest extant reference to Edom is the Papyrus Anastasi VI 51-61 (ANET^2: 259), dated to the eighth year of the pharaoh, probably Merenptah.

In Edom the changing archaeological account of settlement patterns is somewhat the reverse of what it is in Moab and points north. Excavations across the Arabah at Timnah showed that the distinctive 'painted Edomite pottery' (now called 'Midianite' or, better, 'Hejaz pottery' was already being produced at the end of the Late Bronze Age. It had seemed reasonable therefore to conclude that Edom was settled with a consolidated political structure, sometime earlier than the emergence of early Israel (Weippert 1971: 133, n. 17). But as indicated above in Chapter 1, the early consolidation of Edom as a territorial state is seriously questioned, after Bennett's excavations at Umm el-Biyarah, Tawilan, and Buseirah. In 1979 Weippert knew of six sites from the area 'between Wadi el-Hasa and approximately et-Tafileh' with Iron I pottery; from the south, however, one site only (Weippert 1979: 26).

It is the Egyptian references to the mountains of Seir and the fact that Edomites are called *Shasu* nomads, in Papyrus Anastasi VI, that provides Weippert with a key for unlocking the process of Israelite settlement. According to a recent reinterpretation of the Balua' stele (possibly 12th century), the Moabites may also be represented as coming from the Shasu (Giveon 1971: 203).

Following the lead of A. Alt (1967), Weippert's explanation of 'the settlement' focuses first on the location of Israelite tribal areas in Cisjordan, that is, outside the realms of the Late Bronze city-states, in the wooded hill country and the northern Negeb. These areas too were inhabited by Shasu, nomadic tent-dwellers who raised small cattle. Each of the biblical patriarchs, who likewise are pictured as tent-dwelling herdsmen, is associated in biblical tradition with one or two urban enclaves surrounded, Weippert asserts, by 'nomadic areas': Jacob at Shechem and Bethel, Abraham at Hebron and Gerar, Isaac at Beersheba. The last named site, however, cannot be called 'urban' as Weippert realized, until well into the Iron Age. Observing the 'essentially peaceful relationship between the nomadic patriarchs and the cities', and seeing that this corresponds exactly to the more recent findings in 'nomadic research', Weippert concludes that the population from which Earliest Israel was formed in Canaan and Transjordan is known in Egyptian texts as Shasu.

> . . . due to a natural increase in population and due to the arrival of other groups in the 13th century, a point was reached in which the traditional nomadic economies were no longer sufficient to feed the *s3sw* population . . . . Only the possibilities of emigration to Transjordan and of 'internal colonization' remained . . . they were now forced to convert to *systematic* agriculture (Weippert 1979: 33-34).

The result was the sudden blossoming of terrace farming in the hill country at the beginning of Iron I and many new settlements and towns in the former Shasu lands at the same time. In brief, the original tribal league, our 'Earliest Israel', was formed largely out of Shasu population already in Canaan; this was the 'Israel' of the Merenptah stele. The arrival of groups bearing the Exodus and Sinai traditions joined the existing alignment and 'apparently effected something like a "conversion"' (Weippert 1979: 33). The result was our Early Israel.

I do not doubt that there may have been *Shasu* who became Israelite, in the thirteenth to twelfth centuries, as a result of 'something like a conversion'. But I think that Weippert's description of Earliest Israel leans too heavily on the Shasu references for explanatory power. Granted that at least some of the Shasu were tent-dwellers who raised small cattle, and that southern Edom especially was 'Shasu-land' (while Shasu are also found as far north as Syria and southern Lebanon), yet 'the documents concerning the Shasu reveal very little about their mode of livelihood'. L. Stager thus objects that Weippert's wandering herdsmen who became village agriculturalists adapted too quickly to sedentary life at the Late Bronze-Iron I transition, all of a sudden building sophisticated agricultural terraces in great numbers, as well as pillared houses (on both sides of the Jordan), employing the Canaanite alphabet, and making pottery (Stager 1985a). The societal mechanism which Weippert suggests for the emergence of Earliest Israel, that is, the sedentarization of nomadic clans followed by over-population, is not the whole story of the process as described from the side of cultural anthropology, the recent 'nomadic research' to which Weippert refers. The pastoralists often became such due to the advent of hard times in the urban centers, thus precipitating withdrawal. E.A. Speiser posited something of the sort behind the tradition of Abraham's migration out of his homeland. 'They desire a better country' is the way one New Testament writer described such ancient worthies (Heb. 11.16).

Stager knows of 'no historical evidence to suggest that Late Bronze Age pastoralists suffered from acute "overpopulation", which in turn led to widespread "starvation"' (Stager 1985a). There is much evidence in fact that Early Israel's problem was just the reverse, repeated decimation of population due to warfare and its aftermath of epidemic plagues, emanating from the urban centers, and the exactions of imperial overlords (Meyers 1978, 1983).

Stager's essay was triggered by the observation of his student F. Yurco (1978) that the four scenes at Karnak flanking the wall stele of Ramesses II's treaty with the Hittites must have been originally Merenptah's. The scenes depict precisely four of pharaoh's enemies which have been defeated according to the Merenptah stele:

> Now that Tehennu (Libya) has come to ruin,
> Hatti is pacified.

The Canaan has been plundered into every sort of woe:
Ashkelon
has been overcome;
Gezer has been captured;
Yano'am is made non-existent.
Israel is laid waste and his seed is not;
Hurru is become a widow, because of Egypt
(translation and structuring provided Stager by Professor Wente).

Here Israel (husband) and Hurru (wife-widow) are a complementary pair. Surely, Stager suggests, neither spouse was ever as small as the three city-states named: Ashkelon, Gezer, Yano'am. Rather, 'on this occasion Israel was sufficiently strong to field a fighting force against Pharaoh's chariotry and infantry, so as to be placed on a par with Hurru' (Stager 1985a).

At the time of the victory ode in the 'Song of Deborah' (Judges 5), which is only slightly later, the people of Yahweh form a loose alignment (probably ten 'tribes') of diverse occupations (pastoralists, village farmers, seamen) with the active core based in the central highlands. 'The most striking contrast between Israel in the time of Merenptah and in the period of the judges seems to be its *diminished* military might . . .', probably caused in part by Merenptah's campaign (Stager 1985a, italics mine). Earliest Israel had been reduced in size, following Merenptah, on its way to becoming Early Israel.

Ethnogenesis?

Implicit in nearly every attempt to explain Israelite beginnings is an assumption of ethnic homogeneity (recently, de Geus 1976), a deeply rooted and widely shared popular identity, for the origin of which the word 'ethnogenesis' has been coined and used with increasing frequency by biblical scholars. Sometimes qualified as 'religious ethnogenesis', whatever it stands for it must have occurred before there was an Early Israel (Weippert 1979: 33). 'Ethnogenesis' is not defined by those who use it, and I have been unable to find any social science pedigree for this very suggestive term, as saying anything helpful about the origin of social structures. It sounds like jargon to one anthropology department head.

It has been forcibly argued, on the other hand, that something very like contrasting ethnicities formed a large part of the background, which had to be affirmed because they could not be entirely eliminated, in the Yahwist revolution (Mendenhall 1973). The prolonged identity crisis posed for scholars by the Habiru/Hebrew question illustrates the situation very nicely. The extrabiblical references to Habiru (Apiru) do indeed range much too widely over space and time to support any blanket equation with biblical 'Hebrew', if the latter must always also be 'Israelites' (Campbell 1960; Mendenhall 1973: 122-41). The Hebrew word for 'Hebrew', on the other hand, would later acquire an ethnic sense, which, however, is hard to find in biblical texts referring to the premonarchy era. If, as others have argued, both Habiru/Apiru and *'ibri* in the premonarchy era indicate socio-political status (better, no such status), then the use of *'ibri* snaps into clear focus. As shown conclusively by N. Gottwald (1979: 419-20), the same biblical sources can have some of the 'Hebrews' as Israelites (1 Sam. 13.19-20; 14.11-12) *and at the same time*, other biblical 'Hebrews' lined up on the side of the Philistines (1 Sam. 14.21-23a; cf. 13.3-7a)! It cannot be mere coincidence that with the consolidation of the great territorial states in Canaan and Transjordan, from the tenth century on, 'Hebrew' as a term with a long pedigree referring to the marginal persons (and dropouts) simply disappears from scripture, except for a handful of occurrences. To be 'Israelite' was now by definition to be citizen of a territorial monarchy with the apparatus to perpetuate itself. That the earlier sense of 'Hebrew' was not entirely lost in the process is clear from the comic portrayal of Jonah, whose confession 'I am an *'ibri*' (Jon. 1.9), one in flight from Yahweh (legitimate authority), is surely a double entendre. It is to a vast reservoir of older Habiru/Hebrew discontent, amply documented in the fourteenth-century Amarna archives and probably illustrated by many fourteenth- to thirteenth-century destruction layers in Cisjordan (including a late one at Shechem), that we may look for many of those who made up the 'tribes' of Earliest Israel.

Tribal History in Archaic Poetry

In a recent trilogy of trail-blazing essays, D.N. Freedman has vigorously pursued the question of historical memory surviving from premonarchical times, in lengthy poems of Genesis through Judges (Freedman 1975; 1976; 1979). The three essays have been reprinted with others of his studies in early Hebrew poetry, and with a leading essay, 'Poetry, Pottery, and Prophecy', that further undergirds the argument (Freedman 1980). Five major poems comprise the corpus, to which may be applied the principles of 'sequence dating', originally at home in archaeology:

The Testament of Jacob (Genesis 49)
The Song of the Sea (Exodus 15)
The Oracles of Balaam (Numbers 23–24)
The Testament of Moses (Deuteronomy 33)
The Song of Deborah (Judges 5)

That these may be understood as premonarchical in all essentials is shown on stylistic and historical-linguistic grounds. The poems are a prime resource for the historian, but they have regularly been misinterpreted or misapplied, through a harmonistic subordination to their prose settings. None of the prose contexts is earlier than the tenth century, and all of them reflect in one way or another the monarchical transformation of Early Israel. Building on the work of W.F. Albright and a number of Albright's students, as well as his own encyclopedic contributions to the study of Hebrew poetry, Freedman seeks to arrange the poems in chronological sequence, not merely in order of composition, but also in order of content. For an earlier date of composition is no guarantee of higher historicity, and a later composition may in fact reflect accurately a considerably earlier situation. The result is two lists (Freedman 1979: 96) which are reproduced below, with summary of Freedman's discussion of content, interspersed with additional observations mostly with reference to the Transjordan scene.

Poem	*Content*	*Composition*
Genesis 49	14th-13th	11th
Exodus 15	13th-12th	12th
Numbers 23–24	12th	11th
Deuteronomy 33	12th	11th
Judges 5	12th	12th

The following proposal for historical reconstruction agrees broadly with B. Halpern's independent appropriation of the same poems (Halpern 1983). The most significant disagreement arises where Halpern clings to a late (eleventh-century) crystallization of the Judah tribe (Halpern, 157-58).

Genesis 49 (14th-13th-century content). Twelve tribes are named here, in the clearest compact witness to Earliest Israel. Though Reuben (v. 3) is 'firstborn' (on which side of the Jordan Reuben lives is not clear), Judah has the most exalted status (vv. 9-12), with no compelling reason for the critic to regard that status as anachronistic.

Joseph is one tribe in vv. 22-26, whether or not limited to the West

Bank is not clear. If Freedman is correct, the Joseph tribe may have ranged on both sides of the Jordan (as reflected in the later prose narratives of the patriarchs), north and south of the Jabboq, in a period prior to formation of the Amorite Kingdoms on the East Bank, and long before the Yahwist league redefined Israelite 'tribal' areas. The period of Late Bronze I, as we have seen, was one of continually shifting population alignments in the 'land of Gilead', amply attested in the results of archaeological surveys.

Simeon and Levi are denounced for their violence (in vv. 5-7), in terms which indicate that they are being evicted from the inter-tribal organization.

What is said of Gad, who apart from families of the Joseph tribe may alone represent an East Bank tribe in Genesis 49, fits very well with what is suggested above regarding the Amorite kingdoms. That is, the defeat of Sihon in the sequel to this era would be greatly facilitated by Israelites already, and for a long time, in residence there, amidst a variegated sedentary population.

This assessment of the contents of Genesis 49 also helps to understand the Moabite King Mesha's ninth-century claim that 'the people of Gad had lived *m'lm* (from ancient times)' in the land of Mesha's recent expansion, that is, north of the Arnon. And if Jephthah's career falls in the 11th century, his argument that 'Israel' had lived alongside the Ammonite *territory* for some three hundred years' could in fact be based on an approximately accurate round number.

The divine name Yahweh is not used in Genesis 49, except in v. 18, in what is generally recognized as a 'liturgical aside'. Other divine names are preferred: El, Shaddai, and probably Ai. The poem describes a pre-Yahwistic El-league situated mostly but not entirely in Cisjordan. It very likely had its center, for some time, in the El-berit sanctuary (Judges 9) at Shechem (Tell-Balata), where a massive 'Fortress-Temple' from the Middle and Late Bronze periods is now well-known (Wright 1965: 80-102). The most intensive Late Bronze occupation in the Cisjordan hill country occurs around Shechem (Campbell 1968).

For a similar reading of Genesis 49 as a twelfth-century composition carrying memory of a thirteenth-century pre-Yahwist, Israel, including 'Joseph', see Seebass (1984).

Exodus 15 (13th-12th-century content). In this poem there is no hint of a tribal confederation. The name Israel does not occur, and there is no connection with patriarchal traditions or promises about the land of Canaan. The horizon of the poem is limited to the southern wilderness, the traditional home of Yahweh. The Song of the Sea links the tradition of the Exodus from Egypt with the crossing of the sea and the march through the wilderness to the holy habitation of Yahweh, 'the sacred mountain of the deity' (Freedman 1979: 89). The mountain, Freedman argues, is in Sinai, not in Canaan.

Four peoples are struck dumb with terror at this demonstration of Yahweh's saving activity on behalf of the 'people' Yahweh has redeemed. The four named (Philistia, Edom, Moab, Canaan) 'can only have coexisted in their established territories during the 12th century BC' (Freedman 1979: 95). With the mounting evidence from archaeological surveys in Transjordan (Chapter 1), the argument wears very well indeed.

Numbers 23–24 (12th-century content). The Oracles of Balaam concern 'Israel' in Transjordan, but there is no tribal roster. The poet's concern does not yet include Canaan. 'Terror-stricken Moab of the Song of the Sea is the focus of attention and its leader summons Balaam to counterpoise his magic to that of Yahweh' (Freedman 1979: 89).

Freedman is not sure of the setting 'in the plains of Moab', which suggests that Moab has been meddling north of its recognized border, the Arnon. The picture of Israel in its tents, dwelling apart, sounds more, to Freedman, like an oasis setting and Exodus 15. We must observe, however, that it was Edom (not Moab) that had to worry about a threat from Israel on its southern boundary. Apparently 'occupation-forces' in the plains of Moab, north of the Arnon, were pretty much hemmed in by a combination of tent-dwelling newcomers (probably more to the east and southeast) and village-farmer sympathizers (surely more on the north). The only threat to Moab, from 'Israel', lay in Moab's expansion to occupy towns north of the Arnon, as argued above. In other words, it appears that the dismantling of Sihon's kingdom in the south only paved the way for Moabite expansion once again, north of the Arnon, in a region yet to be consolidated as 'Reuben'.

Such a reading of the situation also helps to account for the collaboration of the 'elders of Midian' (Num. 22.7) on the side of Moab in the affair. We may assume that Midianite commercial interests were, by this time, counting on Moabite 'protection', against the mounting protest of the expanding Yahwist movement, with its nascent disruption of the caravan trade, soon to be celebrated explicitly in the highlands of Cisjordan (Judg. 5.6-7; Chaney 1983; Boling 1975: 108-109, 116-20). that Midianites were now well represented in the area north of the Arnon is clear from the story of the incident at Beth-Peor (Numbers 25. See Mendenhall 1973: 105-21).

Deuteronomy 33 (12th-century content). This is a form of the 'all Israel' tradition in which Judah has fallen on hard times (v. 7). Freedman turns to the Samson stories and early Sea Peoples' presence to account for Judah's decline. In any case we may assume that the way to Judah's eclipse had been paved, not long before, by Merenptah's campaign. Reuben, wherever situated, seems to be in equally dire straits, if not more so (v. 6). In view of what is now said about Gad's blessed expansionist leadership (vv. 20-21), I suspect that Reuben is still west of the Jordan, where it will only escape a fate like Simeon's by moving east. Simeon appears to have retreated from central Canaan to the northern Negeb (Josh. 19.1-9), after its ouster in Genesis 49. If so, it has now gone under and is passed over in silence, but will retain a place in idealistic prose genealogies. Simeon's place in the league's decision-making is here filled by division of a greatly expanded Joseph, who gets the most expansive treatment (vv. 13-17), for 'the ten thousand of Ephraim', and 'the thousands of Manasseh' (v. 17). We may suspect, therefore, that any remnants of the Amorite kingdoms in Transjordan are also, at this time, about to go under.

How did it come to pass that violent *Levi, evicted from Earliest Israel* along with Simeon in Genesis 49, *is now the zealous keeper of the oracle* and instructor in how to keep Yahweh's covenant? There may be no more important question to ask of early biblical tradition. It is reasonable to think that at least some of the Levitical families made their way to Egypt, after banishment in Genesis 49, there to give birth to two or three most remarkable levitical persons (Moses, Miriam, Aaron). Their accomplishments in re-forming, re-building, the tribe of Levi, so that it became in effect 'palace guard' in the nascent Kingdom of Yahweh led at last to rival priestly houses, already deeply entrenched in both the northern and southern kingdoms after the schism in 921, as cultivators of the prose traditions (Cross 1973: 195-215; Boling 1984).

Judges 5 (12th-century content). In this form of the 'all Israel' tradition, the organization appears to consist of ten territorially-based tribes. Here it is Judah that is most conspicuous for its absence, and we are deep into the Philistine period. Neither mentioned by name nor alluded to, Judah has joined Simeon. But unlike Simeon, Judah will revive to engulf the territory where Simeon had sought to relocate (Josh. 15.20-63).

Two Transjordan constituencies are faulted for not responding to the muster: Gilead (= Eastern Manasseh?), and Reuben. What has become of Gad? Has Moab once again expanded north of the Arnon, so that Gad's earlier residence there is already receding into the *'wlm*, 'ancient times', to which Mesha will refer in the 9th century?

Lack of any mention or allusion to Levi has always been a major crux in the poem. But is the omission of Levi so surprising in a roster of *territorially based* units? If Deuteronomy 33 represents an earlier situation, with Levi already exalted as teacher and keeper of the oracle for 'all Israel' on the move, the Levitical families are now no doubt already dispersed. Levi comes in for neither praise nor blame in Judges 5, I submit, because its members are functioning as muster officers in every other tribe, on both sides of the Jordan, and with very mixed success.

Conclusion

When all is said and done, the returns from archaeology in Jordan plotted and the stories of Moses and his followers restudied, the conclusion is inescapable that Numbers 21ff. cannot be dismissed as pious anachronism. If such were the case, another set of stories must needs be invented, with action centering in the same general locations, to account for the shifting demographic patterns that are reflected in the surveys and excavations, as seen above in Chapter 1. I do not doubt that the later redactors of the stories often had other interests than strictly accurate history-writing in assembling materials as they did. There is much still to be learned, from 'redaction-history', about the reuse and transformation of traditions. As we have seen above, Numbers 21ff. remains a literary and source-critical quagmire. But within the later mix, it should now be clear, a very old memory lingers on—reliably. What has recently come to be called The Yahwist Revolution in Canaan (better now, The Yahwist Reformation of Earliest Israel) scored its first successes in Transjordan, most likely arriving there by way of 'Midian' in the northern Hejaz, to implant the alternative community, Kingdom of Yahweh, east of the Jordan River. Ironically, the Hejaz is also the homeland of the Hashemites, now holding sway over all of Transjordan, thanks especially to the loyalty of bedouin tribesmen, who fill the ranks and furnish many top ranking officers in a highly sophisticated military establishment.

It is now nearly a quarter of a century since the theory of ancient Israel's revolutionary origins was first proposed (Mendenhall 1962). That was, for many, a new angle of vision on what Martin Buber aptly described, as the movement of early Israel, a 'striving for direct theocracy' (Buber 1967). More recently the social sciences have provided methods and perspectives for sharpening the picture of emerging Israel as an 'egalitarian social movement' (Gottwald 1979), yet another helpful angle of vision.

Biblical scholars by and large, however, have taken their bearings from the Deuteronomistic periodization of 'history'. If the Book of Joshua presents ancient Israel in Canaan as the result of *conquest*, while the Book of Judges reflects a prolonged process of *settlement*, scholars have generally opted for one or the other as more 'reliable'. In truth it was never so simply an either/or. It all began as a mutation in the history of religions and polities that occurred first in the Sinai wastelands. The 'conquest' of Transjordan and Canaan was a *settlement* of warring claims, a settlement which denied unlimited divine-right ownership of land and persons to any human being or group. The 'settlement' of Transjordan and Canaan was a *conquest*, the victory of a new conviction, and one that wears very well. The role of ethic and the ecumenical vision that first became functional in human history with Moses and his followers is every bit as desperately needed today, on both sides of the Jordan River, to say nothing of the world-wide warring family of 'nations', if any members of the family are to survive, and if, indeed, mere *survival* is to be worthwhile.

BIBLIOGRAPHY

Aharoni, Y.
1979 *The Land of the Bible*, revised edition; Philadelphia: Westminster.

Aharoni, Y.; Fritz, V.; & Kempinski, A.
1975 'Excavations at Tel Masos (Khirbet el-Meshash): Preliminary Report on the Second Season, 1979', *Tel Aviv* 2/3, pp. 97-124.

Albright, W.F.
1970 'Midianite Donkey Caravans', *Translating and Understanding the Old Testament*, eds. H.T. Frank and W.L. Reed; Nashville: Abingdon, pp. 197-205.

Alt, A.
1967 'The Settlement of the Israelites in Palestine', *Essays on Old Testament History and Religion*, tr. R.A. Wilson; Garden City, NY: Doubdleday, 173-221.

Bachman, H.-G., and Hauptmann, A.
1984 'Zur alten Kupfergewinnung in Feinan und Hirbet en-Nahas im Wadi Arabah in Südjordanien', *Der Anschnitt. Zeitschrift für Kunst und Kultur im Bergbau* 4, pp. 110-23.

Baly, D.
1957 *The Geography of the Bible*, New York: Harper.

Banning, E.B., & Fawcett, C.
1983 'Main-Land Relationships in the Ancient Wadi Ziqlab: Report of the 1981 Survey', *Annual of the Department of Antiquities in Jordan* 27, pp. 291-307.

Barakat, G., ed.
1973 *The Archaeological Heritage of Jordan*, Amman: Department of Antiquities.

Bartlett, J.R.
1970 'Sihon and Og, Kings of the Amorites', *Vetus Testamentum* 20, pp. 257-77.
1973 'The Conquest of Sihon's Kingdom: A Literary Re-examination', *Journal of Biblical Literature* 97, pp. 347-51.

Bawden, G.
1983 'Painted Pottery of Tayma and Problems of Cultural Chronology in Northwest Arabia', in *Midian, Moab, and Edom*, eds. J.F.A. Sawyer and D.J.A. Clines; JSOT Supplement, 24; Sheffield: JSOT, pp. 37-52.

Ben-Arieh, S.
1978 'A Grave from the Late Bronze Age from Tel Jdur', *Qadmoniyot* 11.

Bennett, C.-M.
1979 'Excavations on the Citadel (al-Qal'a) Amman, 1978, Fourth Preliminary Report', *Annual of the Department of Antiquities of Jordan* 23:161-70.
1983 'Excavations of Buseirah (Biblical Bozrah)', in *Midian, Moab, and Edom*, eds. J.F.A. Sawyer and D.J.A. Clines; JSOT Supplement, 24; Sheffield: JSOT, pp. 9-17.

Bimson, J.J.
1981 *Redating the Exodus and Conquest*, JSOT Supplement, 5; Sheffield: Almond.

Biran, A., et al.
1985 *Biblical Archaeology Today*, Proceedings of the International Congress on Biblical Archaeology, 1984; Jerusalem: Israel Exploration Society, Israel Academy of Sciences and Humanities, American Schools of Oriental Research.

Boling, R.G.
1960 '"Synonymous" Parallelism in the Psalms', *Journal of Semitic Studies* 5, pp. 221-55.
1969 'Bronze Age Buildings at the Shechem High Place', *The Biblical Archaeologist* 32, pp. 81-103.
1975a *Judges*, Anchor Bible 6A; Garden City, NY: Doubleday.
1975b 'Excavations at Tananir, 1968', in *Report on Archaeological Work at Suwwanet eth-Thaniya, Tananir, and Khirbet Minha (Munhata)*, ed. G.M. Landes; Bulletin of the American Schools of Oriental Research, Supplemental Studies, 21; Missoula, MT: Scholars, pp. 28-85.
1982a *Joshua*, Anchor Bible 6; Garden City, NY: Doubelday.
1982b 'Levitical History and the Role of Joshua', in *The Word of the Lord Shall Go Forth*, eds. C.L. Meyers and M. O'Connor; Winona Lake, IN: Eisenbrauns, pp. 241-61.

Boraas, R.S.
1971 'A Preliminary Sounding at Rujm el-Malfuf, 1969', *Annual of the Department of Antiquities of Jordan* 16, pp. 31-45.

Boraas, R.S., & Geraty, L.T.
1976 'The Fourth Campaign at Tell Hesban (1974)', *Andrews University Seminiary Studies* 14, pp. 1-16.
1978 'The Fifth Campaign at Tell Hesban (1976)', *Andrews University Seminary Studies* 16, pp. 1-18.

Boraas, R.S., & Horn, S.H.
1969 'The First Campaign at Tell Hesban (1968)', *Andrews University Seminary Studies* 7, pp. 97-117.
1973 'The Second Campaign at Tell Hesban (1971)', *Andrews University Seminary Studies* 11, pp. 1-16.
1975 'The Third Campaign at Tell Hesban (1973)', *Andrews University Seminary Studies* 13, pp. 101-16.

Bright, J.
1956 *Early Israel in Recent History Writing*, Studies in Biblical Theology; London: SCM.
1965 *Jeremiah*, Anchor Bible 21; Garden City, NY: Doubleday.
1981 *A History of Israel*, third edition; Philadelphia: Westminster.

Buber, M.
1967 *Kingship of God*, third edition; tr. R. Scheimann; New York and Evanston: Harper & Row.

Callaway, J.A.
1981 Review of J.J. Bimson, *Redating the Exodus and Conquest* (Sheffield: Almond, 1981), in *The Biblical Archaeologist* 44, pp. 252-53.

Campbell, E.F., Jr
1960 'The Amarna Letters and the Amarna Period. *The Biblical Archaeologist* 23, pp. 2-22; rpt, *The Biblical Archaeologist Reader* 3 (1970), pp. 54-75.

1968 'The Schechem Area Survey', *Bulletin of the American Schools of Oriental Research* 190, pp. 19-41.

Chaney, M.L.

1983 'Ancient Palestinian Peasant Movements and the Formation of Premonarchic Israel', *Palestine in Transition*, eds. D.N. Freedman and D.F. Graf; Sheffield: Almond, pp. 39-90.

Christensen, D.L.

1974 'Num 21.14-15 and the Book of the Wars of Yahweh', *Catholic Biblical Quarterly* 36, pp. 359-60.

de Contenson, H.

1964 'The 1953 Survey in the Yarmuq and Jordan Valleys', *Annual of the Department of Antiquities of Jordan* 8-9, pp. 30-46.

Cross, F.M.

1973 *Canaanite Myth and Hebrew Epic*, Cambridge, MA: Harvard.

Dajani, R.W.

1966 'Jabal Nuzha Tomb at Amman', *Annual of the Department of Antiquities of Jordan* 11, pp. 48-52.

1970 'A Late Bronze-Iron Age Tomb Excavated at Sahab, 1968', *Annual of the Department of Antiquities of Jordan* 15, pp. 29-34.

Dearman, J.A.

1984 'The Location of Jahaz', *Zeitschrift des deutschen Palästina-Vereins* 100, pp. 122-25.

Dornemann, R.H.

1982 'The Beginnings of the Iron Age in Transjordan', in *Studies in the History and Archaeology of Jordan*, ed. A. Hadidi; Amman: Department of Antiquities, pp. 135-40.

1983 *The Archaeology of the Transjordan in the Bronze and Iron Ages*, Milwaukee: Milwaukee Public Museum.

Fohrer, G.

1961 'Eisenzeitliche Anlagen im Raume südlich von Na'ur und die Südwestgrenze von Ammon', *Zeitschrift des deutschen Palästina-Vereins* 77, pp.57-71.

Franken, H.

1969 *Excavations at Tell Deir 'Alla, I*, Leiden: Brill.

1979 *Yadoudeh: The History of a Land*, Leiden: private publication.

Freedman, D.N.

1975 'Early Israelite History in the Light of Early Israelite Poetry', in *Unity and Diversity: Essays in the History, Literature, and Religion of the Ancient Near East*, eds. H. Goedicke and J.J.M. Roberts; Baltimore: Johns Hopkins, pp. 3-35. Rpt in *Pottery, Poetry and Prophecy*, pp. 131-66.

1976 'Divine Names and Titles in Early Hebrew Poetry', in *Magnalia Dei: The Mighty Acts of God*, eds. F.M. Cross, W.L. Lemke, and P.D. Miller, Jr; Garden City, NY: Doubleday, pp. 55-107. Rpt in *Pottery, Poetry and Prophecy*, pp. 77-129.

1979 'Early Israelite Poetry and Historical Reconstructions', in *Symposia*, ed. F.M. Cross. Cambridge, MA: American Schools of Oriental Research, pp. 89-96. Rpt in *Pottery, Poetry and Prophecy*, pp. 167-78.

1980 *Pottery, Poetry, and Prophecy*, Winona Lake, IN: Eisenbrauns.

Freedman, D.N., & Graff, D.F., eds.
1983 *Palestine in Transition: The Emergence of Ancient Israel*. The Social World of Biblical Antiquity Series, 2; Sheffield: Almond.

Galvin, K.F.
1981 'Early State Economic Organization and the Role of Specialized Pastoralism: Terqa in the Middle Euphrates Region', UCLA Ph.D. dissertation, University Microfilms.

Geraty, L.T. et al.
1986 'Madaba Plains Project. Preliminary Report of the 1984 Season at Tell el 'Umeiri and Vicinity'. BASOR Supplement 24, pp. 117-44.

Gese, H.
1985 'Ammonitische Grenzfestungen zwischen *wadi es-sir und na'ur*', *Zeitschrift des deutschen Palästina-Vereins* 74, pp. 55-64.

de Geus, C.J.J.
1975 'The Importance of Archaeological Research into the Palestinian Agricultural Terraces With an Excursus on the Hebrew word *gbi*', *Palestine Exploration Quarterly* 107, pp. 65-74.
1976 *The Tribes of Israel*, Amsterdam: Van Gorcum.

Giveon, R.
1964 Toponymes Ouest-Asiatiques a Soleb. *Vetus Testamentum* 14, pp.239-55.
1971 *Les bédouins Shasou des documents égyptiens*, Documents et Monuments; Orientis Antiqui, 18; Leiden: Brill.

Glueck, N.,
1934 'Explorations in Eastern Palestine I', *Annual of the American Schools of Oriental Research* 14, pp. 1-114.
1935 'Exploration in Eastern Palestine II', *Annual of the American Schools of Oriental Research* 15.
1939 'Exploration in Eastern Palestine III', *Annual of the American Schools of Oriental Research* 18-19.
1949 'Exploration in Eastern Palestine IV', *Annual of the American Schools of Oriental Research* 25-28.
1970 *The Other Side of the Jordan*, second edition. Cambrige, MA: American Schools of Oriental Research.

Gonen, R.
1984 'Urban Canaan in the Late Bronze Period', *Bulletin of the American Schools of Oriental Research* 253, pp. 61-73.

Gordon, R.L. & Villiers, L.E.
1983 'Telul edh-Dhahab and Its Environs Surveys of 1980 and 1982: A Preliminary Report', *Annual of the Department of Antiquities of Jordan* 27, pp. 275-89.

Gottwald, N.K.
1979 *The Tribes of Yahweh*, Maryknoll, NY: Orbis.

Gunn, D.M.
1974 'The "Battle Report": Oral or Scribal Convention?', *Journal of Biblical Literature* 93, pp. 513-18.
1976 'On Oral Tradition: A Response to John Van Seters', *Semeia* 5, pp. 155-61.

Hadidi, A., ed.
1982 *Studies in the History and Archaeology of Jordan I*, Amman: Department of Antiquities.

Halpern, B.
1983 *The Emergence of Israel in Canaan*, Chico, CA: Scholars.

Hanson, P.D.
1968 'The Song of Heshbon and David's NIR', *Harvard Theological Review* 61, pp.297-320.

Harding, G.L.
1953 'An Early Iron Age Tomb at Madeba', *Palestine Exploration Fund Annual* 6, pp. 27-33.

Harding, G.L., & Isserlin, B.S.J.
1953 'A Middle Bronze Age Tomb at Amman', *Palestine Exploration Fund Annual* 6, pp. 14-22.

Hentschke, R.
1977 'Ammonitische Grenzfestungen südwestlich von 'amman', *Zeitschrift des deutschen Palästina-Vereins* 76, pp. 103-23.

Herr, L.G.
1976 'The Amman Airport Excavations, 1976', *Annual of the Department of Antiquities of Jordan* 21, pp. 109-11.
1986 'The Amman Airport Excavations, 1976', *Annual of the American Schools of Oriental Research* 48, Joseph A. Callaway, ed.

Hiatt, J.M.
1981 'Between Desert and Town: A Case Study of Encapsulation and Sedentarization Among Jordanian Bedouin'. University of Pennsylvania. Ph.D. dissertation, University Microfilms.

Hopkins, D.C.
1985 *The Highlands of Canaan*, Sheffield: Almond.

Ibach, R.D., Jr
1976 'Archaeological Survey of the Hesban Region', *Andrews University Seminary studies* 14/1, pp. 119-26.
1978a 'Expanded Archaeological Survey of the Hesban Region'. *Andrews University Seminary Studies* 16/1, pp. 201-13.
1978b 'An Intensive Surface Survey at Jalul', *Andrews University Seminary Studies* 16/1, pp. 215-22.
1981 'The Hesban Region Survey', Grace Theological Seminary: Winona Lake, IN: (Prepublication ms).

Ibrahim, M.M.
1972 'Excavations at Sahab, 1972', *Annual of the Department of Antiquities of Jordan* 17, pp. 23-36.
1974 'Second Season of Excavations at Sahab, 1973'. *Annual of the Department of Antiquities of Jordan* 19, pp. 55-61, Pls. XII-XXII.
1975 'Third Season of Excavations at Sahab, 1975 (Preliminary Report)', *Annual of the Department of Antiquities of Jordan* 20, pp. 69-82.

Ibrahim, M., Sauer, J. & Yassine, K.
1976 'The East Jordan Valley Survey, 1975', *Bulletin of the American Schools of Oriental Research* 222, pp. 41-66.

Ingraham, M.L. et al.
1980 'Preliminary Report on a Reconnaissance Survey of the Northwestern Province (with a Note on a Brief Survey of the Northern Province)', *Atlal: the Journal of Saudi Arabian Archaeology* 5, pp. 59-84.

Jacobs, L.K.
1983 'Survey of the South Ridge of the Wadi 'Isal, 1981', *Annual of the Department of Antiquities of Jordan* 27, pp. 245-73.

Jobling, W.J.

1980 'Preliminary Report on the Archaeological Survey Between Ma'an and 'Aqaba', *Annual of the Department of Antiquities of Jordan* 25, pp. 105-11.

1983 'The 1982 Archaeological and Epigraphic Survey of the 'Aqaba-Ma'an Area of Southern Jordan', *Annual of the Department of Antiquities of Jordan* 27, pp. 185-95.

Kafafi, Z.

1979 'Late Bronze Age Pottery in Jordan (East Bank) 1575-1200 B.C.', unpublished M.A. thesis, University of Jordan.

Kalsbeek, J. & London, G.

1978 'A Late Second Millenium B.C. Pottery Puzzle', *Bulletin of the American Schools of Oriental Research* 232, pp. 47-56.

Kautz, J.R.

1981 'Tracking the Ancient Moabites', *The Biblical Archaeologist* 48, pp. 27-35.

Kerestes, T.M. et al.

1978 'An Archaeological Survey of the Three Reservoir Areas in Northern Jordan, 1978', *Annual of the Department of Antiquities of Jordan* 22, pp. 108-35.

King, G., Lenzen, C.J., & Rollefson, G.O.

1983 'Survey of Byzantine and Islamic Sites in Jordan. Second Preliminary Season Report, 1981', *Annual of the Department of Antiquities of Jordan* 27, pp. 385-436.

Kitchen, K.A.

1964 'Some New Light on the Asiatic Wars of Ramesses II', *Journal of Egyptian Archaeology* 50, pp. 47-70.

Knauf, E.A.

1984 'Abel-Keramim', *Zeitschrift des deutschen Palästina-Vereins* 100, pp. 119-21.

Landes, G.M.

1961 'The Material Civilization of the Ammonites', *The Biblical Archaeologist* 24, pp. 66-86. Rpt *Biblical Archaeologist Reader* 2 (1964), pp. 69-88.

Lenzen, C.J. & Mcquitty, A.

1983 'A Preliminary Survey of the Irbid-Beit Ras Region, Northwestern Jordan', *Annual of the Department of Antiquities of Jordan* 27, p. 656.

Leonard, A., Jr

1979 'Kataret es-Samra: A Late Bronze Age Cemetery in Transjordan?', *Bulletin of the American Schools of Oriental Research* 234, pp. 53-65.

1981 'Kataret es-Samra: A Late Bronze Age Cemetery in Transjordan', *Annual of the Department of Antiquities of Jordan* 25, pp. 179-95.

Ma'ayeh, F.C.

1960 'Recent Archaeological Discoveries in Jordan', *Annual of the Department of Antiquities of Jordan* 4-5, pp. 11-16.

MacDonald, B.

1982 'The Wadi el-Hasa Survey 1979 and Previous Archaeological Work in Southern Jordan', *Bulletin of the American Schools of Oriental Research* 245, pp. 35-52.

1983a 'The Wadi el Hasa Archaeological Survey 1982: Phase III. ASOR Newsletter (January 1983),' pp. 5-8.

1983b 'The Late Bronze and Iron Age Sites of the Wadi El Hasa Survey, 1979', in *Midian, Moab, and Edom*, eds. J.F.A. Sawyer & D.J.A. Clines; JSOT Sup, 24. Sheffield: Almond, pp. 18-28.

1984 'The Wadi el-Hasa Archaeological Survey', in *The Answers Lie Below*, ed. H.O. Thompson, New York and London: Lanham, pp. 113-28.

MacDonald, B., Banning, E.B., & Paulish, L.A.

1980 'The Wadi el Hasa Survey, 1979: A Preliminary Report', *Annual of the Department of Antiquities of Jordan* 24, pp. 169-83, Pls. CIII-CX.

MacDonald, B., Rollefson, G.O., & Roller, D.W.

1982 'The Wadi El Hasa Survey 1981: A Preliminary Report', *Annual of the Department of Antiquities of Jordan* 26, pp. 117-30.

MacDonald, B. et al.

1983 'The Wadi el Hasa Archaeological Survey 1982: A Preliminary Report', *Annual of the Department of Antiquities of Jordan* 27, pp. 311-23.

Marfoe, L.

1979 'The Integrative Transformation: Patterns of Socio-Political Organization in Southern Syria', *Bulletin of the American Schools of Oriental Research* 243, pp. 1-42

Mattingley, G.L.

1983 'The Exodus-Conquest and the Archaeology of Transjordan: New Light on an Old Problem', *Grace Theological Journal* 4/2, pp. 245-62.

Matthews, V.H.

1979 *Pastoral Nomadism in the Mari Kingdom (ca. 1830-1760 B.C.)*, American Schools of Oriental Research Dissertation, 3.

McCarter, P.K., Jr

1980 'The Balaam Texts from Deir 'Alla: the First Combination', *Bulletin of the American Schools of Oriental Research* 239, pp. 49-60.

McCreery, D.W.

1978 'Preliminary Report of the A.P.C. Township Archaeological Survey', *Annual of the Department of Antiquities of Jordan* 22, pp. 150-62.

McGovern, P.E.

1980 'Exploration in the Umm ad-Dananir Region of the Baq'ah Valley', *Annual of the Department of Antiquities of Jordan* 24, pp. 55-67.

1981 'The Baq'ah Valley Project 1980', *The Biblical Archaeologist* 44, pp. 126-28.

1982a 'Exploring the Burial Caves of the Baq'ah Valley in Jordan', *Archaeology* 35/5; pp. 46-53.

1982d 'Baq'ah Valley Project 1981', *The Biblical Archaeologist* 45, pp. 122-24.

1983 'Test Soundings of Archaeological and Resistivity Survey Results at Rujm al-Henu', *Annual of the Department of Antiquities of Jordan* 27, pp. 105-37.

McGovern, P.E., Harbottle, G., & Wnuk, C.

1982c 'Late Bronze Age Pottery Fabrics from the Baq'ah Valley, Jordan: Composition and Origins', *MASCA Journal* 2, pp. 8-12.

Mellaart, J.

1962 'Preliminary Report on the Archaeological Survey on the Yarmuk and Jordan Valley for the Point Four Irrigation Scheme', *Annual of the Department of Antiquities of Jordan* 6-7, pp. 126-57.

Mendenhall, G.E.
1962 'The Hebrew Conquest of Palestine', *The Biblical Archaeologist* 25, pp. 66-87; Rpt *The Biblical Archaeologist Reader* 1970, pp. 100-20.
1973 *The Tenth Generation*, Baltimore: Johns Hopkins.

Meshel, Z.
1975a 'On the Problem of Tell el-Kheleifeh, Elath and Ezion-geber', *Eretz Israel* 12, pp. 49-56.
1975b 'Yotvata', *Hadashot Arkiologiyot* 26, pp. 50-51 (in Hebrew).

Meyers, C.
1978 'The Roots of Restriction: Women in Early Israel', *The Biblical Archaeologist* 41, pp. 91-103.
1983 'Procreation, Production, and Protection: Male-Female Balance in Early Israel', *Journal of the American Academy of Religion* 51, pp. 569-93.

Miller, J.M.
1979a 'Archaeological Survey South of Wady Mujib', *Annual of the Department of Antiquities of Jordan* 23, pp. 79-92.
1979b 'Archaeological Survey of Central Moab: 1978', *Bulletin of the American Schools of Oriental Research* 234, pp. 43-52.

Mittmann, S.
1970 *Beiträge zur Siedlungs- und Territorialgeschichte des nördlichen Ostjordanlandes*, Wiesbaden: Otto Harassowitz.
1973 Num 20,14-21—eine redaktionelle Komposition, in *Wort und Geschichte: Festschrift für K. Elliger*, eds. H. Ges and H.P. Rüger; Neukirchen: Neukirchener Verlag. 143-49.

Newman, M.L., Jr
1962 *The People of the Covenant: A Study of Israel from Moses to the Monarchy*, New York: Abingdon.

Noth, M.
1941 'Das Land Gilead als Siedlungsgebiet israelitischer Sippen', *Palästina Jahrbuch* 37, pp. 50-101.
1960 *The History of Israel*, second edition; tr. P.R. Ackroyd; New York: Harper & Row.
1968 *Numbers*, tr. J.D. Martin; Philadelphia: Westminster.

Oláváarri, E.
1965 'Sondages a 'Aro'er sur l'Arnon', *Revue biblique* 72, pp. 77-95.
1969 'Fouilles à 'Aro'er sur l'Arnon. Les Niveaux du bronze intermédiaire', *Revue biblique* 76, pp. 230-59.
1975 'Aroer', in *Encyclopedia of Archaeological Excavations in the Holy Land I*, Englewood Cliffs, NJ: Prentice-Hall, pp. 98-100.

Parr, P.
1982 'Contacts Between Northwest Arabia and Jordan in the Bronze and Iron Ages', *Studies in the History and Archaeology of Jordan I*, ed. Adnan Hadidi. Amman: Department of Antiquities, pp. 127-33.

Parr, P.J., Harding, G.L., & Dayton, J.E.
1970 'Preliminary Survey in N.W. Arabia 1968', *Bulletin of the Institute of Archaeology, University of London*, Nos. 8 & 9.

Pritchard, J.G.
1964a 'Excavations at Tell es-Sa'idiyeh (Preliminary Report)', *Annual of the Department of Antiquities of Jordan* 8-9, pp. 95-98.
1964b 'Reconnaissance in Jordan', *Expedition* 6/2, pp. 3-9

1965a 'A Cosmopolitan Culture of the Late Bronze Age', *Expedition* 7/4 pp. 26-33.

1965b 'Excavations at Tell es-Sa'idiyeh', *Archaeology* 18, pp. 292-94.

1966 'Tell es-Sa'idiyeh, Jordan', *Archaeology* 19, pp. 289-90.

1980 *The Cemetery at Tell es-Sa'idiyeh*, University Museum Monograph, 41; University of Pennsylvania: Philadelphia.

von Rabenau, K.

1978 'Ammonitische Verteidigungsanlagen zwischen Hirbet el-Bisara und el-Yadude', *Zeitschrift des deutschen Palästina-Vereins* 94, pp. 46-55.

von Rad, G.

1966 *Deuteronomy*, tr. D. Barton; Philadelphia: Westminster.

Rast, W.E., & Schaub, R.T.

1974 'Survey of the Southeastern Plain of the Dead Sea, 1973', *Annual of the Department of Antiquities of Jordan* 19, pp. 5-53.

Redding, R.W.

1981 'Decision Making in Subsistence Herding of Sheep and Goats in the Middle East'. University of Michigan Ph.D. dissertation, University Microfilms.

Redford, D.B.

1982 'A Bronze Age Itinerary in Transjordan (Nos. 89-101 of Thutmose III's List of Asiatic Toponyms), *Journal for the Society of Egyptian Archaeology* 12/2, pp. 55-74.

Reventlow, H.G.

1963 'Das Ende der ammonitischen Grenzfestungskette', *Zeitschrift des deutschen Palästina-Vereins* 79, pp. 127-37.

Rothenberg, B.

1972 *Timna*, London: Thames & Hudson.

Rothenberg, B., & Glass, J.

1983 'The Midianite Pottery', in *Midian, Moab, and Edom*, eds. J.F.A. Sawyer & D.J.A. Clines; JSOT Supplement, 24, pp. 65-124.

Rowton, M.B.

1973a 'Urban Autonomy in the Nomadic Environment', *Journal of Near Eastern Studies* 32, pp. 201-15.

1973b 'Autonomy and Nomadism in Western Asia', *Orientalia* 42, pp. 247-58.

1974 'Enclosed Nomadism', *Journal of the Economic and Social History of the Orient* 17, pp. 1-30.

1976a 'Dimorphic Structure and the Problem of the 'Apiru-'Ibrim', *Journal of Near Eastern Studies* 35, pp. 13-20.

1976b 'Dimorphic Structure and Topology', *Oriens Antiquus* 15, pp. 17-31.

1976c 'Dimorphic Structure and the Tribal Elite', *Studia Instituti Anthropos* 28, pp. 219-57.

1977 'Dimorphic Structure and the Parasocial Element', *Journal of Near Eastern Studies* 36, pp. 181-98.

Saller, S.J., & Bagatti, P.

1949 *The Town of Nebo (Khirbet el-Mekhayyat)*, Jerusalem: Franciscan.

Sawyer, J.F.A., & Clines, D.J.A., eds.

1983 *Midian, Moab and Edom*, JSOT Supplement, 24; Sheffield: JSOT.

Seebass, H.

1984 'Die Stammessprüche Gen 49,3-27', *Zeitschrift für die alttestamentliche Wissenschaft* 96, pp. 333-50.

Simons, J.
1959 *The Geographical and Topographical Texts of the Old Testament*, Leiden: Brill.

Smend, R.
1970 *Yahweh War and Tribal Confederation*, tr. M.G. Rogers; Nashville & New York: Abingdon.

Smith, R.H.
1973 *Pella of the Decapolis I*, Wooster, OH: College of Wooster.

Stager, L.E.
1976 'Agriculture', *The Interpreter's Dictionary of the Bible, Supplement*, pp. 11-13.
1985a 'Merenptah, Israel, and Sea Peoples: New Light on an Old Relief', *Eretz-Israel* 18: pp. 56*-64*.
1985b 'The Archaeology of the Family in Ancient Israel', *Bulletin of the American Schools of Oriental Research* 260, pp. 1-35.

Summer, W.A.
1968 'Israel's Encounter With Edom, Moab, Ammon, Sihon and Og According to the Deuteronomist', *Vetus Testamentum* 18, pp. 216-18.

Thompson, H.O.
1972 'The 1972 Excavation of Khirbet Al-Hajjar', *Annual of the Department of Antiquities of Jordan* 17, pp. 47-72.
1973 'Rujm al-Malfuf South', *Annual of the Department of Antiquities of Jordan* 18, pp. 47-50.
1977 'The Ammonite Remains at Khirbet al-Hajjar', *Bulletin of the American Schools of Oriental Research* 227, pp. 27-34.

Thompson, T.L.
1974 *The Historicity of the Patriarchal Narratives*, Beiheft zur Zeitschrift für die alttestamentliche Wissenschaft, 133; Berlin: Walter de Gruyter.

Tushingham, A.D.
1972 *The Excavations at Dibon (DHIBAN) in Moab*, Annual of the American Schools of Oriental Research, 40.

Van Seters, J.
1972 'The Conquest of Sihon's Kingdom: A Literary Examination', *Journal of Biblical Literature* 91, pp. 182-97.
1975 *Abraham in History and Tradition*, New Haven and London: Yale.
1976 'Oral Patterns or Literary Conventions in Biblical Narrative', *Semeia* 5, pp. 139-54.
1980 'Once Again—The Conquest of Sihon's Kingdom', *Journal of Biblical Literature* 99, pp. 117-19.

de Vaux, R.
1938 'Chronique: Exploration de la région de Salt', *Revue biblique* 47, pp. 348-425.
1941 'Notes d'histoire et de topographie Transjordaniennes', *Vivre et Penser I*, Paris: J. Gabalda.
1961 *Ancient Israel*, tr. J. McHugh; New York: McGraw-Hill.

Ward, W.A.
1964 Cylinders and Scarabs from a Late Bronze Temple at Amman, *Annual of the Department of Antiquities of Jordan* 8-9, pp. 47-55.
1966 'Scarabs, Seals and Cylinders from two tombs at Amman', *Annual of the Department of Antiquities of Jordan* 11, pp. 5-18.

1973 'A Possible Link Between Egypt and Jordan During the Reign of Amenhotep III', *Annual of the Department of Antiquities of Jordan* 18, pp. 45-46.

Weippert, M.

The Settlement of the Israelite Tribes in Palestine. Studies in Biblical Theology II/21; London: SCM & Naperville, Ill.: Allenson.

1979 'The Israelite "Conquest" and the Evidence from Transjordan', in *Symposia*, ed. F.M. Cross. Cambridge, MA: American Schools of Oriental Research, pp. 15-34.

Wright, G. E.

1965 *Shechem: Biography of a Biblical City*, New York: McGraw-Hill.

1971 'What Archaeology Can and Cannot Do', *The Biblical Archaeologist* 34.70-76; Rpt *The Biblical Archaeologist Reader 4*, E.F. Campbell & D.N. Freedman, eds.; Sheffield: Almond (1983), pp. 65-72.

1982 'Introduction', in R.G. Boling, *Joshua*, The Anchor Bible 6; Garden City, NY: Doubleday, pp. 1-88.

Yassine, Kh.

1984 *Tell el Mazar I: Cemetery A*, University of Jordan.

Yurco, F.

1978 'Merenptah's Palestinian Campaign. Abstract of discussion at the 1979 meeting of the Society for the Study of Egyptian Antiquities', *Journal for the Society of the Study of Egyptian Archaeology* 8, p. 70.

Zayadine, F.

1973a 'Recent Excavations at the Citadel (Al Qal'a) Amman 1967', *Annual of the Department of Antiquities of Jordan* 23, pp. 17-30.

1973b 'Late Bronze Age', in *The Archaeological Heritage of Jordan*, Amman: Department of Antiquities, pp. 19-21 and Map 6.

INDEX

INDEX OF BIBLICAL REFERENCES

Genesis
12–50 39
31.48 44
49 58-59, 61

Exodus
15 58-59

Numbers
20.14–21.35 41
20.14-21 45
20.18 26
21–23 47
21 46, 48
21.14-21 51
21.14-15 48
21.21-35 44
21.21-25 45
21.22 45
21.24 41
21.27-31 48, 49
21.27-30 41
21.28-29 51
21.29 45
21.33-35 43
21.33 43
21.25 45
21.35 45
22–36 52
22–25 50
22.1 52
22.2–24.25 47
22.7 60
23–24 58-59
25 47
26.63 52
31.8 28
31.12 52
33.48-50 52
35.1 52
36.13 52

Deuteronomy
1–3 43
1.4 42
2 47
2.1–3.11 41
2.4-8 26
2.18 48
2.26-37 45
2.27-29 45
3.1-11 43
3.1 43
3.3-10 45
3.10 42
3.11 43
4.43 42
4.46 41
11.19-26 45
31.4 41
33 58, 61-62
34.1 52
34.8 52

Joshua
2.10 41
9.10 41-42
11.1 28
12 42
12.4b-5 42
12.4 42
12.5 42
13.11 42
13.12 42
13.31 42
13.32 52
15.20-63 62
19.1-9 61
20.8 42

Judges
5 58, 62
5.6-7 61
5.14 38
6–8 28
9 59
10.17 44
11 52
11.12-28 41
11.12-22 45
11.19-26 45
11.24 52
11.29 44
11.33 35

1 Samuel
13.3-7a 57
13.19-20 57
14.11-12 57
14.21-23a 57

1 Chronicles
5.11 42
6.71 42

Psalms
137.7 47

Jeremiah
48.1-47 46
48.45-46 45
48.45a 46, 48
48.47 46
49.1-6 46
49.7-32 46

Ezekiel
35 47
47.13-23 46

Obadiah 47

Jonah
1.9 57

Hebrews
11.16 55

INDEX OF AUTHORS CITED

Aharoni, Y. 27, 29, 65
Albright, W.F. 28, 58, 65
Alt, A. 44, 54, 65

Bachmann, H.-G. 28, 65
Bagati, P. 30, 73
Baly, D. 42, 65
Banning, E.B. 20, 24, 65, 71
Barakat, G. 13, 65
Bartlett, J.R. 41-44, 46, 65
Bawden, G. 28, 65
Ben-Arieh, S. 27, 65
Bennett, C.M. 24, 26, 28, 65
Bimson, J.J. 9, 66
Boling, R.G. 29, 39, 42-43, 49, 51, 52, 61, 66
Boraas, R.S. 29, 32, 66
Bright, J. 39, 66
Buber, M. 63, 66

Callaway, J.A. 9, 66
Campbell, E.F. 57, 59, 66
Chaney, M.L. 61, 67
Christensen, D.L. 48, 67
Clines, D.J.A. 73
de Contenson, H. 16, 67
Cross, F.M. 27, 44, 61, 67

Dajani, R.W. 29, 67
Dayton, J.E. 72
Dearman, J.A. 42, 67
Dornemann, R.H. 28, 30, 67

Fawcett, C. 20, 65
Fohrer, G. 29, 67
Franken, H. 34, 44, 67
Freedman, D.N. 57-60, 67-68
Fritz, V. 65

Galvin, K.F. 12, 68
Galling, K. 44
Geraty, L.T. 7, 13, 32, 35, 68
Gese, H. 29, 68
de Geus, C.J.J. 56, 68
Giveon, R. 27, 54, 68
Glass, J. 73
Glueck, N. 11, 14, 25, 27, 29, 51, 68
Gonen, R. 22-24, 68
Gordon, R.L. 30, 68
Gottwald, N.K. 40, 57, 63, 68
Graff, D.F. 68
Gunn, D.M. 46, 68

Hadidi, A. 68
Halpern, B. 58, 69
Hanson, P.D. 50, 69
Harbottle, G. 71
Harding, G.L. 30, 69, 72
Hauptmann, A. 28, 65
Hennessey, B. 29
Hentschke, R. 29, 69
Herr, L.G. 29, 69
Hiatt, J.M. 69
Hopkins, D.C. 13, 69

Ibach, R.D., Jr 32, 34, 47, 69
Ibrahim, M.M. 14, 16, 25, 69
Ingraham, M.L. 26-27, 69
Isserlin, B.S.J. 69

Jacobs, L.K. 20, 69
Jobling, W.J. 26-27, 70

Kafafi, Z. 11, 70
Kalsbeek, J. 27, 70
Kautz, J.R. 14, 70
Kempinski, A. 65
Kerestes, T.M. 18, 70
King, G. 20, 70
Kitchen, K.A. 53, 70
Knauf, E.A. 21, 35, 70
Kraus, H.-J. 44

LaBianca, Ø.S. 29, 30
Landes, G.K. 29, 30
Lapp, P.W. 14
Lenzen, C.J. 7, 13, 18, 20, 70
Leonard, A., Jr 70
London, G. 27, 70

Ma'ayeh, 29, 70
MacDonald, B. 7, 24-25, 27, 70-71
Marfoe, L. 13, 71
Mattingly, G.L. 7, 14, 17, 20, 71
Matthews, V.H. 12, 71
McCarter, P.K., Jr 44, 71
McCreery, D.W. 7, 71
McGovern, P.E. 29, 71

McQuitty, A. 13, 18
Mellaart, J. 16, 71
Mendenhall, G.E. 28-29, 40-41, 43, 51, 56-57, 61, 63, 72
Meshel, Z. 27, 72
Meyers, C. 55, 72
Miller, J.M. 14, 52, 72
Mittmann, S. 14, 16-18, 51, 72
Mortensen, P. 14

Newman, M.L., Jr 38, 72
Noth, M. 10, 37-39, 41-45, 50, 72

Olávarri, E. 30, 72

Parr, P. 26-28, 72
Paulish, L.A. 24, 71
Pritchard, J.G. 16, 72

Rabenau, K. von 29, 73
Rad, G. von 43-44, 73
Rast, W.E. 21, 73
Redding, R.W. 12, 73
Redford, D.B. 35, 73
Reventlow, H.G. 29, 73
Rollefsok, G.O. 20, 24, 70-71
Roller, D.W. 24, 71
Rothenberg, B. 27-28, 73
Rowton, M.B. 12, 73

Saller, S.J. 30, 73
Sauer, J. 14, 16, 25, 69
Sawyer, J.F.A. 73
Schaub, R.T. 21, 73
Seebass, H. 59, 73
Simons, J. 48, 74
Smend, R. 38, 74
Smith, R.H. 16, 74
Speiser, E.A. 55
Stager, L.E. 13, 55-56, 74
Summer, W.A. 74

Thompson, H.O. 29-30, 74
Thompson, T.L. 39, 74
Tushingham, A.D. 30, 74

Van Seters, J. 39, 44-47, 49, 74
de Vaux, R. 11, 30, 44, 74
Villiers, L.E. 30, 68

Ward, W.A. 74
Weippert, M. 30, 47-51, 53-56, 75
Wnuk, C. 71
Wright, G.E. 10, 59, 75

Yassine, Kh. 14, 16, 21, 25, 69, 75
Yurco, F. 55, 75

Zayadine, F. 75

INDEX OF GEOGRAPHICAL AND PLACE NAMES

Abel-Keramim 35
Amarna 37, 41
Amman 13, 30, 35
Amman citadel 27, 28
Ammon 46
Aqaba 11, 26
Ar 48, 49, 50
Arabah 11, 27, 28, 52
Arad 47
Arnon Heights 50
Arnon R. 11, 37, 41, 42, 48, 52, 60
Ash-Shorabat 25
Ashkelon 56
Ashtaroth 42, 43

Baal-Peor 47, 50
Balua‘ 54
Baq‘ah valley 29, 30
Bashan 42, 43
Beersheba 54
Beit Ras 13, 17, 18
Beqa‘ valley 13
Bethel 54
Beth-Peor 61
Bilas 34
Bosrah 24
Bozra 37, 51
btrt 53
Buseirah 24, 54

Cisjordan (hill country) 13, 22, 23, 35, 54, 59, 61
Coral Island 27

Der‘a 42
Dibon 41, 49

Edom(ite) 21, 24, 26, 27, 28, 37, 45, 46, 60
Edrei 42, 43
Elat 27
el-Al 30
el-Buneiyyat South 34
el-Buneiyyat North 34
el-Medeineyeh al-Thamad 41-42
el-Misna‘ 48, 53
et-Tafileh 54

Galilee 28

Gerar 54
Gezer 56
Gilead 44
Gilgal 44
Golan 42

Ham 18
Hawshiyan 20
Hazor 23
Hebron 54
Hejaz 26, 27, 28, 63
Hermon 41
Heshbon 41, 49, 50
Hormah 47
Ḫuḫḫa 43

Iktanu 32
Irbid 13, 17, 18

Jabboq R. 11, 14, 28, 37, 41, 42, 44
Jabesh-Gilead 44
Jahaz 41
Jalul 32
Jebel Druze 42
Jebel Nuzha 28
Jebel Utud 26
Jericho 44
Jezirat Faroun 27
Jordan Valley 14, 17, 18, 21, 22, 25, 38

Karnak 55
Kataret es-Samra 21
Kerak 20, 21
Kh. Ain el-Ghuzlan 25
Kh. al-Hajjar 29, 30
Kh. el-Medeineyeh 53
Kh. el-Mekhayyat 30
Kh. es-Suq 34
Kh. Jel‘ad 44
Kh. Umm ad-Dananir 29
Kh. Umm el-Idham 30
Kheleifeh 27
King's Highway 47
Kufr Yuba 18
Kuga 43

Lachish 23
Lejjun 53

Ma'an 26
Madaba 41, 47, 49
Madaba Plains 13, 32, 34, 50
Madaba tomb 30
Madon 28
Maqarin Dam 18
Mari 26
Marqa Airport 29, 42
Mizpeh-Gilead 44
Moab 11, 14, 17, 21, 45-49, 52, 60
Moab, Kingdom 22, 30
Moab, Plains of 51, 52, 60
Moab(ite) plateau 11, 17, 21, 24
Mount Hermon 42
Mount Sirion 41
Mount Nebo 30
Mudawwara 26
Mugha'ir Shuy'ab 27

Naur 34
Negeb 26, 28, 47, 54, 61
Nuzi 39

Pella 16, 21, 37, 43, 51
Philistia 60

qryt-syhn 49
Qurayya 26, 27, 28

Rabbah 53
Rabbat Ammon 29, 30
Rakbat Umm-Edgeyer 26
Ramoth-Gilead 44
Ras Rihab 25
Reshuni 44
Rujm al-Malfuf South 29
Rujm el-Henu 29

Sahab 29
Sahem el-Jolan 42
es-Salt 11
Salecah 42
Salkhad 42
Seir 37
Shechem 54, 57, 59
Sinai 28

Tabahat Fahl 16
Tabuk 26
Talal Dam 18
Tawilan 24, 27, 54
Tayma 26, 27, 28
Tell Ashtarah 42
Tell Balata 59
Tell Deir 'Alla 44
Tell Hesban 32, 41, 47
Tell Jalul 47
Tell Jdur 27
Tell el-Kharaz 26
Tell el-Umeiri, East 32
Tell el-Umeiri, West 32, 34, 35
Tell es-Sa'idiyeh 16
Tell Masos 27
Tell Mazar 21
Tell Safut 29
Tell Sal 18
Telul edh-Dhahab 30
Timna 26, 27
Tishbeh-Gilead 44

Ugarit 41
Um Guwei'ah 27
Umm al-Sarab 20, 32
Umm el-Basatin 34
Umm el-Biyarah 24, 54

Wadi Arab 18
Wadi el-Hasa 11, 21, 24-27, 52
Wadi el-Heidan 42
Wadi el-Wala 42
Wadi eth-Thamad 25, 42
Wadi 'Isal 20
Wadi Mujib 11, 12, 17, 20-22, 28, 30, 35, 48, 52
Wadi Rajib 16
Wadi Rumman 26
Wadi Ziglab 20

Yadoudeh 34
Yanoam 56
Yarmuq R. 11, 14, 17, 18, 35, 41
Yotvata 27

Zarqa R. 11, 14, 17, 18, 20, 28, 30
Zered R. 11, 24